BECOMING WELLSTONE

BECOMING WELLSTONE

*Healing from Tragedy
and Carrying On My Father's Legacy*

Paul David Wellstone Jr.

HAZELDEN®

Hazelden
Center City, Minnesota 55012
hazelden.org

Library of Congress Cataloging-in-Publication Data

Wellstone, Paul David, Jr., 1965-
  Becoming Wellstone : healing from tragedy and carrying on my father's legacy / Paul David Wellstone Jr.
      p. cm.
  Includes bibliographical references.
  ISBN 978-1-61649-445-2 (softcover) -- ISBN 978-1-61649-456-8 (ebook)
  1. Wellstone, Paul David--Influence. 2. Wellstone, Paul David--Political and social views. 3. Wellstone, Paul David--Family. 4. Wellstone, Paul David, Jr., 1965- 5. Mental health insurance--Law and legislation--United States. 6. Lobbying--Washington (D.C.) 7. Fathers and sons--Minnesota. 8. Fathers--Minnesota--Death. 9. Bereavement--Psychological aspects. 10. Adjustment (Psychology) I. Title.
  E840.8.W457W45 2012
  328.73'092--dc23
                                                        2012025473

16 15 14 13 12   1 2 3 4 5 6

Cover design: David Spohn
Front cover photo: Author photo
Back cover photo: Brian Peterson/Star Tribune
Interior design and typesetting: Madeline Berglund

For my parents, Paul and Sheila,
and my sister Marcia
and for Mary McEvoy, Tom Lapic,
and Will McLaughlin

Ten years later, your
spirits all still burn bright.

CONTENTS

ACKNOWLEDGMENTS

Above all I want to thank my kids, Cari and Keith, for being the inspirations of my life. Without them, this book would never have happened. I hope they'll take pride in this book—and show it to their children and grandchildren. I want to thank my wife, Leah, for her support and love and above all for making me happy. I also want to thank my parents for bringing me up to believe that even when something is hard—*especially* when something is hard—it can be worth doing. I never thought I could write a book. Throughout the work on this project I heard their voices telling me to stick with it and I would surprise myself. I hope that my parents and my sister can be proud of what I've been able to share here of the Wellstone family story and I hope it continues to inspire people.

Nick Motu, the publisher at Hazelden, must have thought I was crazy when I contacted him earlier this year to say I wanted to do a book—and wanted to have it ready in October to mark the ten-year anniversary of the plane crash no one in Minnesota will ever forget. Thanks to Nick and his entire team for being flexible and creative partners in this project, especially Sid Farrar and Peter Schletty. Their input and advice shaped the manuscript in so many ways. If the book is good, credit goes to them. If it falls short, that's on me.

I also have to single out my partners in the fight on parity, especially Holly Merbaum, Ellen Gerrity, and Carol McDaid, for their tireless efforts and commitment to mental health and addiction and also for their friendship and support. Same goes to Patrick Kennedy and Jim Ramstad.

Finally, I'm trying to keep this short so I'll just add a shout out to my brother, Mark, and his beautiful family, Jill, Bode, and Collette, to Steve and Sarah for a connection that was inexplicable yet made all three of us so clear about what we could do together with the Wellstone Center in the Redwoods, and to Gwen for all her support and for being a great mom. Ciara and Alex, glad to have you in my life. Rick Kahn, I know why my dad loved you.

THE CRASH

he call came late that morning. My parents had left the St. Paul airport at 9:37 a.m. on a quick hop of a flight to a funeral in Eveleth, Minnesota, but something had gone wrong. The Beechcraft King Air A100 eleven-seater carrying my parents, my sister, and three staffers could not be located on radar. I didn't know what to think. No one did. I had already slipped into a zombie-like state and didn't even know it yet. It was as if I watched someone else pay the check at Bakers Square and get into the car and drive off, then later walk into my father's Senate campaign headquarters in St. Paul and exchange blank, uncomprehending looks with the people there, most of them in tears. It was as if I watched someone else pick up my brother and drive him home, then listened to the radio with him when an announcement came on that the Beechcraft King Air A100 had gone down. It was as if I watched someone else drop my brother off and then continue on alone, driving north from the Twin Cities and finally up from the Duluth area on little Highway 53 leading up toward the Iron Range town of Eveleth.

That was when I saw the smoke. It was a dark, dirty plume cutting up into the slate-gray background of heavy cloud cover. I knew right away what I was seeing. It was the plane. It had to be. Back when I was a competitive wrestler, I remember feeling my stomach flip-flopping and doing cart-wheels, but nothing like this. If I let myself focus on the riot in my stomach or focus on any one thing at all, I knew I'd have no chance of getting through those hours. Instead, I concentrated on moving forward. I pulled off the highway and turned on a side road that brought me closer to the plume of smoke. By this time a light rain was falling and it was dark. I saw the flashing lights of a police barricade blocking my way forward and did not think twice before hitting the gas and driving around it so I could head farther up the road. No one knew who I was. I parked my car and got out. In the distance I could see a fire burning. It must have been after 5 p.m. by then. Law enforcement was all around, and finally an officer came up to me and told me to leave. I had to tell him who I was.

"I'm very sorry, Mr. Well—" the officer started to say, but I was having none of it.

"What's going on here?" I shouted.

Even as I was shouting, I was still staring at the flaming plane wreckage, which no one was approaching.

"Why aren't you *doing* anything?" I complained. "Why can't you put out this fire?"

"It's too dangerous," the officer said. "The jet fuel is highly combustible. It poses a—"

"That's bullshit!" I said, cutting him off.

Law enforcement had mounted surveillance cameras within range of the crash site when they first arrived on the scene and then withdrawn to a safe distance. They took me to a trailer they had set up where they were monitoring the surveillance video. Suddenly what had only been blurry confusion at a distance took vivid form. I could see a tight close-up of the flaming plane. The impact of the crash had pushed everyone to the front compartment. I could see that. I could also see shadows that I knew were people, shadows that represented my father, my mother, and my sister.

"Nothing can be done, Mr. Wellstone," they kept telling me.

The words settled over me like dark ice. I was a Wellstone. I'd been raised a Wellstone. My father's father was a Russian Jew who fled just before the Bolshevik Revolution, which claimed the lives of his parents. My grandfather was a man of action, a doer, passionate about the need to fight for justice. He passed that passion and that belief in action on to my father, who grew up in Virginia as the smallest kid around but who was never, ever one to get lost in the crowd. As a wrestler, my dad was unstoppable and ended up undefeated, champion of the Atlantic Coast Conference for his weight division. As a professor at Carleton College in Minnesota, after earning his Ph.D. at age twenty-four, he threw himself into campus activism, organizing protests and speaking out against campus ties to corporate interests. My brother, sister, and I were brought up to think and consider and learn, but above all, always to do. Now I was frozen in a trailer watching my life as I knew it end. All I kept hearing was the voice of officers telling me there was nothing to do, nothing to do, nothing to do.

I did my best to fight through the numbness and disbelief that overwhelmed me in that trailer near the plane. Back at the crash site later that week, I spotted a small flower that made me think of my father. I found a spot for it in the branches of a tree not far from where the plane had gone down and placed the small flower there, intending it as a kind of message for my father. He could not be gone. He was too strong a presence, too strong a man. It was simply unimaginable that, just like that—like *that*—he could suddenly no longer be there. I was sure he had been thrown from the plane and was still lying around somewhere nearby. I was convinced he would hop up and walk around and see the small flower I had left for him. That wasn't the last time I returned to the crash site. I went back again. Many times. But I could never find that flower again or any sign of it, let alone any trace of my father.

After that, I did a lot of nothing—days, weeks, months of nothing. I went home and stayed home. My neighbors were kind enough to take turns bringing me a hot dish every night. I might not have eaten for days on end otherwise. I was incapable of shopping. I was incapable of cooking. I was incapable of doing much of anything. I received a package one day that was so big and strange that I had to open it up. It turned out that they had somehow sent me all the items from the crash by mistake. The shock and disbelief knifed through me again as I pulled out the charred remnants of a watch and a burnt, partially melted wedding ring. Then I came upon a burnt "Wellstone" campaign button that smelled so strongly of jet fuel, it made me sick to my stomach. Getting a whiff of that smell made me so dizzy, I toppled over and collapsed to the ground. To this day, I feel queasy whenever I smell jet fuel.

I opened almost no mail after that. It would pile up like snowdrifts. I will always carry a vivid recollection from this period of my startled, disconnected reaction when I saw a van show up one afternoon so someone in a jumpsuit with a name tag and a logo on the back could pop out and turn off my water. I hadn't paid my bill. I hadn't even opened my bill. Then someone else showed up with a foreclosure notice. I hadn't made my house payments either. I hadn't made any payments. I just didn't give a shit about anything. I lost twenty pounds. My eyes had a hollow, empty look. It was time to get out of there. I would never be free in Minnesota to find a way forward to my future. Too many memories. Too many associations. Too many bizarre, disturbing experiences, like the Halloween day when I heard a radio DJ announce, "This Halloween I'm going to go as a dead person. I'm going to put on a Paul Wellstone mask." Too many people making a fuss on those rare occasions when I ventured out and tried to pay with a credit card at a restaurant or supermarket and they saw the name "Paul D. Wellstone."

So I left Minnesota and moved to the Santa Cruz Mountains in northern California, where I could just be Dave. That was when my healing began. As I will explain in this book, I did not find a house in my adopted home state, a house found me. I was on Amigo Road in Soquel, low on the ridge of mountains that divides the Pacific Ocean from Silicon Valley. One thing led to another, and I felt myself pulled up to a house high on the ridge looking down, a house surrounded by redwoods and the healing energy they bring. I made this my home for many years to come and turned it into a place of spiritual power, a place of recovery and growth, a place where I could have the time I needed to heal and rejuvenate, and ultimately to take on new challenges—like the writing of this book and the journey it both represented and opened up for me and, I hope, many of you as well.

CHAPTER 1

GROWING UP WELLSTONE

---

*I*n one sense I was like most kids growing up: I got into a lot of arguments with my dad about haircuts.

"No!" he would say.

"Yes!" I would say.

"You don't need a haircut!" he would say.

"But Dad, I want one!" I would say.

For my entire childhood, my father had a wild, bushy head of hair—a full-on "Jewfro." He was so proud of his hair and would tend it constantly with a pick he kept in his back pocket, like J.J. on the 1970s TV show *Good Times* ("Dyn-o-mite!"). My old man loved long hair.

"It's okay to be different, David," he would tell me. "You don't need a haircut. Just because everyone else does something doesn't mean you have to. And anyway, you look better with your hair longer."

1

His message was: *Think for yourself. Don't just go around with the crowd. Never be afraid to take an unpopular stand. Always question authority.*

I hear stories about kids growing up in the 1960s whose parents had loose, free-form ideas about the values they instilled in their children. My parents were nothing like that. They were constantly asking themselves questions about what sort of moral education to provide for me, and later my sister, and then my kid brother. They thought about this stuff every single day. They talked about it with us all the time, especially to me as the oldest. From the time I was very young, my father always wanted to bring me along when he met with disadvantaged people so I could see for myself what was going on in the world.

My parents got married young and were both just twenty years old when I was born in March 1965. My father was a graduate student then at the University of North Carolina at Chapel Hill, writing his Ph.D. dissertation called "Black Militants in the Ghetto: Why They Believe in Violence." The FBI sent in agents to seize the dissertation. He eventually got it back, but it took some work—and he was rattled. Even when I was very small, I always had a sense of people being mad at my father for some reason or of him setting them off, but never of him backing down in his beliefs.

Later he told me the story of following a trail of dead rabbits on the road, which people in North Carolina knew led to a meeting of the Ku Klux Klan, then showing up and confronting the KKK. That led to a tense standoff. He denounced the men in white bedsheets and one of them told him, "Let me show you what we do with troublemakers like you," and then flipped up a cover on the back of a pickup truck to reveal a pile of guns. That was the end of that standoff.

I guess being athletic ran in the family. My father had gone to UNC on a wrestling scholarship and went undefeated on his way to winning the Atlantic Coast Conference title for his weight class. I had a wrestling mat in my crib. I was always very active. I have hazy, half-formed early memories of being on the UNC campus with my dad when I was a toddler. Even as a little kid I could throw a Frisbee, and when my dad would take me to campus with him, that was a big hit with the other students. They would all crowd around to see me do it again, this little two-year-old flinging a Frisbee sidearm. That really impressed them!

We always had music playing in our tiny apartment in Carrboro, North Carolina. Simon and Garfunkel released the album *Parsley, Sage, Rosemary and Thyme* in 1966 and once the movie *The Graduate* came out in 1967, "Scarborough Fair" was a hit single and you heard it everywhere. I can remember sitting in a tiny little wooden rocking chair hearing that song over and over and trying to memorize the words. "Blowin' in the Wind" and other early Dylan songs were the soundtrack to my childhood. Are you kidding me? A little Jewish guy singing about injustice and ticking off anyone older than thirty? My dad's love of Dylan might have even had something to do with him later ending up as a college professor in Minnesota, where Dylan was born and grew up.

I had some issues when I got old enough for day care in Chapel Hill. Let's just say that Richard Nixon's election as president in 1968 didn't go over real well in our household. My parents did not need Woodward and Bernstein reporting in the *Washington Post* or the Watergate scandal in the early 1970s to know where they stood on Nixon. My parents were shocked that the American people could elect such a person. They talked about it all the time. So when Bobbi, my day care provider, started talking about President Nixon one day, I knew just what to say back to her: "Nixon is a fascist pig!"

This outburst caused a major brouhaha. My parents had a hard time explaining to me why the things we talked about at home together could not always be repeated to other people. North Carolina had of course voted for Nixon, as did the entire South, except for Texas and the states that went for segregationist George Wallace.

My parents did not readily use language like "fascist pig." They tried to be more tolerant of differing viewpoints, as my father made clear much later when he was in the U.S. Senate and formed friendships with even some very conservative Republicans. But 1968 was a traumatic year for my parents, as it was for the entire nation. When word came in early April that Martin Luther King Jr. had been assassinated on a balcony at the Lorraine Motel in Memphis, Tennessee, my father was more upset than I had ever seen him. He was sobbing and crying and finally had to run outside. He was soothed somewhat by the eloquent words spoken shortly afterward by Senator Robert Kennedy, who implored African Americans not to let the tragic death fill them with bitterness.

"For those of you who are black and are tempted to be filled with hatred and mistrust of the injustice of such an act, against all white people, I would only say that I can also feel in my own heart the same kind of feeling. I had a member of my family killed, but he was killed by a white man," Bobby Kennedy said.

Two months later, Bobby was dead too. He was gunned down after midnight at the Ambassador Hotel in Los Angeles by Sirhan Sirhan the night he won the California primary. My father found out the next morning and again he was inconsolable. Within a five-year span, Martin Luther King and Jack and Bobby Kennedy had all been murdered. As a kid, I only knew that my father was sobbing once again, but at some level I understood. My father was struggling not to turn bitter and hateful, and to use this tragedy to strengthen his resolve even more, always to fight for the underdog, the disadvantaged, the powerless.

What I will never forget about life in North Carolina was the heat. Never again have I lived anywhere with that kind of heat. I remember it being so hot that my mom and I would fry an egg on the sidewalk in front of our tiny apartment, sunny-side up. My dad would put me on his lap and let me drive the car up the driveway to the apartment, just to keep me distracted. I was never satisfied with just moving forward. I'd twist the wheel to try to turn the car off the driveway, and he'd just laugh and straighten the wheel back.

WE START A NEW LIFE IN MINNESOTA

One of my first memories of Minnesota was that no one could understand me. My Southern accent was too thick. My father was hired as a political science professor at Carleton College in Northfield, Minnesota, starting in September 1969. He was only twenty-five years old and became the youngest professor they had ever hired. He was not about to do what most of the Carleton faculty did and live on the same street as a bunch of college professors. He wanted to be with the people. We found a house on the blue-collar side of town on a quiet street with a lot of families. As soon as I could, I ran outside to join a ball game. None of the other kids could figure out what I was trying to say.

"Foul ball!" I kept repeating.

"What?" they all said.

My father was an iconoclast, but when it came to our home life, we could not have been a more traditional family. June Cleaver had nothing on my mother. She was always there at home to look after us and drive me to everything. We were one of those families where you could pretty much guess what we were eating on a given night based on the day of the week. My mom had a rotation, so Tuesday night was spaghetti, burgers on Friday night, and so on. My mother was fiercely protective of our dinnertime, so if the phone rang while we were eating—as it often did—she was not always pleasant. Even though it was usually someone wanting my father's help, she would pick up the phone and give the caller a piece of her mind.

"We're having dinner now," she would say. "Don't you know it's six o'clock now, dinnertime? Call back in an hour."

I'd walk home for lunch every day during elementary school and my mother would be there to cook me lunch. It would be just the two of us. She was always my sounding board to talk about how I was feeling. She was my emotional frame of reference. We talked about things in a different way than I could with my father, who was always a man on a mission. My dad never liked to go to the movies or play games. His attitude was always, *Why would I want to go sit in a theater for two hours? Or sit down over a game board? Why would I want to waste that time? There's work to be done! Causes to be fought for! People to help!*

My mother taught me how to play Yahtzee and we would play that for hours. I loved it because the dice made a lot of noise and I could beat my mother sometimes. She also loved cards and we would play gin rummy, crazy eights, go fish. Movies were more of a special occasion, since we didn't have a lot of money for that kind of thing. I remember when *The World According to Garp* came out later and my mother and I saw it together. It felt a little odd to sit through some of those scenes with her, since that movie had some very adult themes, but Robin Williams played a wrestler, and by then I was a wrestler, too—like my dad—so it was a given that we would see it.

My mother and father came from very different backgrounds. His father was a Jewish writer who emigrated from Russia. Her parents were Southern Baptists from Appalachia. She grew up in Kentucky coal-mining country. My father liked to say that when they met on the beach in Ocean City, Maryland, both of them only sixteen, it was as if he could hear the song "Two Different Worlds" playing in the air. But none of that mattered much in their marriage, and it didn't make a difference to us kids. I didn't feel Jewish and I didn't feel Christian. We never really participated in organized religions. It was a nonissue in our family.

The religious people my father admired were figures like Mother Teresa, people who rolled up their sleeves and devoted their lives to helping others. We would talk in the family sometimes about Catholicism, but only in the context of practical help for the poor. My father was impressed with the work Mother Teresa did with orphans and with the sick and elderly in Calcutta, India, starting in 1950. He had worked with a lot of nuns on various social issues since he was young. So I always saw a connection between religion and social justice, but it was a connection that was meant to encourage you, to inspire you, to get you busy making a difference in your own life. It did not matter what organization or faith you joined. What mattered was how you chose to live your life, the deeds you did or did not do. That was the spirituality I was brought up with.

I GET TO KEEP MY BLOCKS

My dad may not have been a tall man, standing five-foot-five, but he was strong as an oak and always carried me on his shoulders. I felt so safe and secure up there—most of the time. I remember sitting up on his shoulders for a Vietnam

War protest in Minnesota when I was very young, and suddenly there was chaos all around us. I was so small, my mother was furious with my old man for insisting on bringing me along. She was glaring at him, hand on hip, as we got ready to leave the house.

"You better not get arrested!" she said.

My mother's palpable fear made the event seem that much more exciting to me. She was against the war, too. That went without saying. Opposition to the war in Vietnam was in many ways centered in Minnesota, where our senator Gene McCarthy had decided to run for president in 1968 as an antiwar candidate. My mother was just worried about my father getting into trouble. She was very nervous about what might happen. She loved his passion, but worried sometimes about his judgment.

I had a great time at the protest. From up on my father's shoulders, I had a view of everything and I loved seeing so many people gathered together. There were speakers, but as a kid, I didn't pay much attention to them. What did make an impression on me was the chanting.

"Hell, no, we won't go!" I heard all around me.

And of course, "Make love, not war!"

But the one that stuck with me the most was "1-2-3-4, we-don't-want-your-fucking-war."

Then the rally broke up in a hurry. My father and I, like everyone else at the protest, had to beat a retreat, especially when the police dispersed the crowd with plumes of tear gas, turning it into a scene of chaos. Dad was fast and had no problem pulling me down from his shoulders and carrying me as he ran full tilt to make sure he heeded my mother's warning and did his best not to get arrested. That might not have been the best way to get in good with his colleagues on the political science faculty either.

Soon after that Vietnam protest, my parents were surprised to see that I had written on my blocks. Then they saw what I had written and were even more surprised: A "1" and a "2" and a "3" and a "4"—that didn't faze them—and then a "we" and a "don't" and a "want" and an "a" and a "fucking" and a "war."

You should have seen the look on my mother's face when she saw those blocks!

"Paul!" she cried out.

My dad came over to look and could not hold back a chuckle. Soon my mother had to smile, too. Talk about a chip off the old block! They let me keep those blocks. They didn't even make me wash off what I had written.

"But don't write on your blocks anymore!" my mother scolded me, fighting back a laugh as she turned away.

IF LOVING SPORTS MAKES YOU ALL-AMERICAN, NO ONE COULD TOP US

Like any working-class neighborhood in the United States during the 1970s, our street in Minnesota was always buzzing with activity, usually centered on sports. It was great having a dad who was young and fit and scrappy. He was in his mid and late twenties those first years in Minnesota. After he came home from work, he would grab a football and the

two of us would toss that back and forth like two kids playing. He and I took on everyone in two-on-two football. At
first they laughed at us. Here we were, my five-foot-five dad
and me a little guy, taking on some big, beefy older neighborhood kids who were used to steamrolling anyone who
came along. But my dad and I usually won. We had our set
plays that we practiced ahead of time, and we were quicker
and more disciplined than the neighbor kids.

We had a Catholic church down at the end of our idyllic
street, which probably explains why we had so many large
families on our block with lots of kids running around all the
time. There was always a game going on. You could tell the
season by the game that was under way: hockey in winter,
either outside or at the rink two blocks away; and out front
on our block, baseball in spring and summer, and football
in fall and winter. We also made up our own games, like one
called Green Hornet. This game was played just as it was
getting dark. The object was to wait for a car to roll up the
street, keeping a close eye on the headlights, and hold off as
long as you could before making a dash and sprinting across
the street just before the headlight would shine on you.

One of my favorites games was Wiffle ball, because you
could wail on that thing and it would never go so far that you
lost the ball. Wiffle ball was big on our street. We organized
teams and kept accurate statistics, and of course we knew our
exact batting averages at all times. We would have tourna-
ments with all the kids on the block with special rules, like hitting the ball onto the roof was a home run. The best was on
Sundays, when the street would be full of cars parked for

Sunday mass. We had a special rule that hitting a car was an automatic out, making it a lot more challenging on Sundays!

When dinner was ready at night, my mother would walk just outside the front door and scream, "David!" Wherever I was, within a block, I had better make sure I heard that and come running home right away.

My sister, Marcia, was four years younger than me, and I worked hard at being a good big brother to her. That is, I teased her as much as I could, but always looked out for her and tried to be there for her. If boys were after her, I'd be protective. That's what big brothers do, right? She was a good runner and ran both cross country and track. As I said, I tried to be a good brother, but I was also a kid messing around and doing the things kids do. One time I got tied up with my friends and got home late. I had missed Marcia's cross-country meet and that was a big, big deal to my parents. We always went together as a family to watch whenever one of us was competing. My parents were not at all happy with me for missing Marcia's meet. They sat me down for a good talking to about that and I learned my lesson. From then on, I was a regular watching my sister's races. She was one of the top runners on the varsity team when she was only in eighth grade and was also a natural at gymnastics from an early age. I remember going to Sibley Elementary School and being awed at the unbelievably long tumbling runs she did that made you dizzy just watching, as well as her other top event, the balance beam.

My little brother, Mark, was seven years younger than me, which meant that if anything ever happened when we were playing, it was always on me. It would usually end up with him getting hurt and crying, and my father yelling at me, "If he's hurt, so help me!" Even so, we had a lot of fun. I grew up playing football and hockey with Mark in the driveway. We could play Wiffle ball for hours. We would go through the entire lineup of the Minnesota Twins, player by player, calling out the name in our best imitation of Bob Casey, the famous Twins PA announcer at Metropolitan Stadium, drawing it out the way he did, "Nowww baaaaating, Kennnn Lannn-dreaux," or "Nowwwwwww baaaaaating, Royyy Smallllll-ey." That would keep us entertained for the longest time. Whichever one of us was up to bat would hop around to swing left-handed or right-handed, depending on which Twins hitter's name we would call out.

My dad would also take me to see the Twins in the early 1970s when the Chicago White Sox were in town so we could see Richie Allen play. He batted .316 in 1973. (I love these stat guys who try to say batting average is overrated as a statistic. Let's see one of them hit .316 in the big leagues over an entire season.) We'd go sit in the outfield and root for Richie Allen to hit an inside-the-park home run.

That same year was a great one for our football team, the Minnesota Vikings, "the Purple People Eaters" led by quarterback Fran Tarkenton. They opened the season with a home win over the Oakland Raiders, even though George Blanda kicked three field goals, and from there they were on a roll: Nine straight wins to start the season. They finished the regular season 12–2 and earned a home playoff game against the Billy Kilmer–era Washington Redskins at Metropolitan

Stadium. That's the same stadium where my dad and I would see the Twins, and we figured we'd go out and pick up some tickets and see the game. I was incredibly fired up. Then we got there and discovered that the only available tickets were being scalped for way more than their face value.

"Son, we just can't pay that much money," my father had to tell me.

I was devastated. It was a huge lesson for me. By then we couldn't even watch the game on TV. I was so disappointed that I didn't even feel much better when the Vikings won 27–20. But eight days later, when they followed that up with a 17–10 road win over the Dallas Cowboys to earn a trip to the Super Bowl, I was thrilled. I had just read Roger Staubauch's new autobiography, *First Down, Lifetime to Go.* The Cowboys of those years had such an aura. It was amazing that our guys could even beat them. The Vikings held their annual spring training camp at Carleton College every year when I was a kid, which gave me added incentive to go along with my father to lift weights. We'd often see a group of football players in there.

I used to go regularly to the little gym at Carleton along with my dad and a group of professors, including Mike Casper, his best friend and a physics professor, and Dave Appleyard, a mathematics professor. They would run three to five miles regularly, and often I would tag along. Back then, my dad ran every day of the week and often lifted weights afterward.

It's hard to explain the importance that wrestling had in my house growing up. As I said earlier, I literally had a wrestling mat in my baby crib. For my father, wrestling represented deliverance. He'd grown up in the Washington, D.C., area as a "tough" kid, as he put it, known to get into some scrapes. Not until wrestling did he find a sense of direction. Not until he found wrestling—or wrestling found him—did everything come together for him. He believed in the kind of energetic hard work that would wear out just about anyone else, but since he was always fit and strong, he could handle that pace every day of his life. He wanted me and my sister and brother to follow in his footsteps by being active and fit because he saw that as essential preparation for life. Later on, new staffers learned fast that if the senator was on the road, he had to have time in his schedule to get in a good workout first thing in the morning. If he didn't get his daily hour-long exercise, he would feel so thrown off physically, he'd start to think he was coming down with a cold.

I was more into running than wrestling when I was a kid. I was a fast little squirt and even went to the Junior Olympics one year, winning silver medals in the half-mile and mile. My dad was so proud, he couldn't stop smiling for a week. I did not start wrestling myself until later, when my father took a sabbatical from Carleton and the family relocated to Columbia, Maryland, for a year. The sabbatical was for my father, so he could do book research, but uprooting myself and moving to an entirely different corner of the country turned out to be a good thing for me, too. I could be a real smart-ass as a kid. I freely admit it. Hell, I can be a smart-ass even now, but at least I've learned a thing or two about not taking myself too seriously. I'm the first one to laugh at myself. As a fifth-grader in Maryland, however, maybe I was scared or insecure, but I pushed it way too far. I would ask so many annoying questions in class, crack jokes, or just be a pain in the ass. I was forever pushing my teachers to the edge of their patience with my whole smart-ass routine, and the school administration had to come down hard on me. My parents were called in to that school every second or third week and, believe me, I heard about that from them. They were not at all happy with me for getting kicked out of class.

The year we lived in the Washington, D.C., area, twenty-five miles away from the Capitol, was an important chance for my father to renew old acquaintances and make new friends. He loved Minnesota and the work he was able to do there, but he was someone who had to always be learning, gaining new skills, developing new ideas. That's why he loved to meet other people who shared his passions. One of the few people who was as intensely committed to grassroots organizing as him was a man named George Wiley, whose National Welfare Rights Organization had eighty chapters and more than 125,000 members around the country.[1] George was also living in Washington at that time, and he and my father became good friends.

George went sailing out on Chesapeake Bay that August in a twenty-three-foot boat along with his two children, Daniel and Maya. The waters turned rough. George slipped and fell overboard and his children tried in vain to pull him back out of the water, but couldn't save him. My dad heard the news and was devastated. He came home that day and could not stop crying. George was a good friend, and it was such a freak accident, so hard to understand. He deeply admired George's approach to political action, his commitment to hard work and careful organizing, and the way he reached out to both blacks and whites. For the remainder of his life, my father was always very uneasy any time he went out on the water.

One afternoon sticks out in my mind from that year in Maryland. I used to play tennis on a court near the apartment complex where we lived. The area was almost entirely African American, and that block with the tennis court was a tough neighborhood. A group of black kids surrounded the tennis court where I was playing that day and had their eyes on a guy much older than me who they wanted to beat up. I did what came naturally: I got the hell out of there! I took off running back to our apartment. When I got home, my dad wanted to know what was going on, so I had to tell him, and he marched right over to that playground so he could set things right. I didn't like this idea at all. I was sure it was going to get ugly. I followed along behind him, dreading what would happen. When we showed up, the same group of tough-looking guys were still there, menacing the older guy.

"What's going on?" my father demanded.

They all just stared at him. He was one man, five-foot-five, and they were a whole group of guys, big and strong and angry looking, who did not look at all ready to talk. Silence dragged out. I was getting more scared by the second. Then my father did something that truly surprised me. He turned around and left. He walked away. There was nothing he could do there and he knew it. I learned that day that even my father knew that sometimes you just have to walk away.

Over the years, people have often asked me, "What made your father the way he was? Why was he always such a fighter? Why did he react so viscerally to injustice?" The truth is, I really can't pinpoint the reasons—and he himself could not have told you either. I don't think it had much to do with his upbringing or family history. That was just the way he was wired. It was an inner compulsion. When he saw a wrong, he could not let it go. He needed to try to make it right. Most people just turn away. My father never turned away. He always called it like it was and jumped into the fray.

~ CHAPTER 2 ~

MY DAD THE TROUBLEMAKER

t was embarrassing growing up with a dad like mine. That's the simple truth of the matter. When you're a kid, you don't always want to call attention to yourself. Sometimes you just want to fade into the background. That idea was incomprehensible to my old man. He did not fade. He did not function in the background. He did not believe in either, not for him, and not for his son. For him, one of the imperatives of life was to always be looking for ways to get involved and make a difference in other people's lives, even if that might put you in risky situations now and then. I just wanted to live my life. I was always wondering why my father had to go out and make a big stink all the time.

"Dad, this is embarrassing," I would tell him.

"You have to stand up for what you believe in, son," he would say. "Always. It's important."

My father's insistence on always fighting for what he believed in got him in trouble on occasion. I'll never forget the day he came home in January 1974 after finding out he had, in effect, been fired from Carleton College. Oh, he knew he was taking a lot of chances with his unapologetic defiance of the entire system. He did not believe that a political scientist should be concerned only with dry, academic research, especially at that time and place. He believed it was just as valid a pursuit to focus his energies on actual grassroots political organizing and getting his students out the door and active and involved. He'd already been barred from ever teaching again at the University of North Carolina at Chapel Hill for upsetting traditional ideas of the role of a political scientist. Faculty members there had tried to get him fired for allegedly teaching a "black power" class. My father had always been a controversial presence on the Carleton College campus, culminating in a months-long review of his performance—and even though he was braced for bad news, still when the word came, it shocked him deeply.

My father was never one to spend much time hanging around the house. That was not his style. Suddenly, after the firing, he was always around. The house we were living in then, built in the late nineteenth century, had a basement lined with heavy limestone walls. That's where my bedroom was. Working with my friend Greg, I made a little office for my dad on the other side of the laundry room next to my bedroom. We put up a crude two-by-four wall glued to the floor, then finished the room with blond plywood. I was eight years old then. Up until this time, my father was hardly ever in there. But now he would come home early and sit in his office for hours at a time and would sometimes pull out a cigar and light that up. You knew he was there, that's for sure, when the smell of those cigars wafted out. I'd walk in and try to talk to him.

"Whatcha doin', Dad?" I'd ask.

He'd be puffing on a cigar, staring at the wall. It would take him a minute to look over at me.

"Thinking," he'd answer finally.

He was extremely fearful, worried he would not be able to provide for us. Dad knew he was a good teacher—he'd just received a round of student evaluations that established him as a clear favorite of Carleton students—but that did not appease the timid administrators. Nor was it any guarantee of future job options. He knew that if he lost this job, he might have serious trouble finding another teaching position anywhere in the country. Carleton had put him on notice that he had only one year left to teach—and the news left him "shaken," as he put it in his book.

"Right away, I thought of Sheila and our three children," he writes in *The Conscience of a Liberal*. "Where would we go? What were we going to do? I felt tremendous fear and guilt. This experience gave me a real feeling for why many people put up with so much and are so passive. You do not want to lose your job. You have to put bread on the table and prioritize for your family. That is why most people, as someone once said, are more concerned with making a living than with making history."[2]

By this point, my father had been working for several years with the poor people of Rice County, mostly mothers who were on welfare and didn't have many options to improve their lives. He helped found the Organization for a Better Rice County (OBRC), which pushed for basic services for the poor like day care and health care. He would regularly go down to the county seat of Faribault and meet with these women and get them thinking like activists. Often he would bring me along. This might not have been what certain faculty members at Carleton College considered the best way for a political science professor to spend his time, but my father disagreed. He thought an ongoing study of politics in action was exactly how he could gain more expertise and then pass that on to students—and to me, his son.

That is one of my first memories of going for a drive with my father—to Faribault, Minnesota, the Rice County seat, so he could meet with the leaders of this group trying to organize. What I remember most about the day is not wanting to go. I dreaded going out there to the poorest end of the county. I told my dad no, I wasn't going. We know who won that argument. For my father it was very important that the whole family show up, not just him, so it was part socializing, part organizing.

Sure enough, it was a balmy summer afternoon in Minnesota, and once we got out there I had a lot of fun. I was a city kid, and getting out in the country like that meant whole huge fields for me to play in. They let me shoot a pellet gun, and I fired that thing all over the place and climbed up silos. They even let me drive a tractor, which I think was as entertaining for them as it was for me. I got it going just fine, but then I couldn't make it stop. Tractors just go. "What do I do?" I kept crying out. They laughed and laughed at that. There were games, and a barbecue with corn on the cob and burgers and hot dogs. Somewhere along the way, my father found time to talk with the women about organizing, including a nurse named Patti Fritz, who would go on to be elected to the Minnesota House of Representatives.

There was an awkwardness for me just in being there and having the strong feeling that my dad was not like other parents. He always had to take a stand, to be the squeaky wheel. Although I was embarrassed by my dad's actions, I saw that others viewed him differently. By tagging along to these kinds of events, I was able to witness the admiration and respect people had for him, almost love, whether it was the families on welfare in Rice County or anyone else he helped, and it had an impact on me. I could see with my own eyes that these people really trusted him and respected him for doing what he didn't have to do.

"Dr. Wellstone treats everyone as his equal, no matter what their status in life," wrote one of the OBRC leaders, Therese Van Zuilen, in a letter to Carleton officials that was also published in the student paper after my dad was fired. "He has (for the first time in their lives, maybe), given incentive to old people, some who can't even read or write, to speak up clearly and express themselves to city councils, county commissioners, etc., to let their needs be known. He gave them dignity by listening, with interest, to them and becoming involved with their problems. He needs no vote of confidence except to say that you'll lose a great teacher and community leader if you let him go."

CARLETON BACKS DOWN

The leaders of the Carleton political science department had to have expected some controversy over their decision to fire my father. They were, after all, political scientists. It was their job to understand political forces. They were paid to predict how political conflicts would play out. But in the case of dumping my father, they had obviously miscalculated. The Rice County mothers were not the only ones incensed at the news of the "early tenure decision" in his case, as the powers that be liked to put it. Students were also up in arms—and happy to take action on my father's behalf.

As a January 24, 1974, article in the student paper, *The Carletonian,* put it in summing up the case, "Wellstone has been noted for his vocal criticism of the Vietnam War, and of college practices relating to pedagogy and education diversity. . . . Nevertheless, this is hardly the end of Paul Wellstone at Carleton College. A detailed and concise response to the charges leveled against him is forthcoming. Someone with as colorful and dynamic a career at Carleton as Paul Wellstone is not likely to slip quietly away."

No he was not. He had not been dubbed "the professor of political activism" by his students for nothing. His course "Social Movements and Grassroots Organizing" was not mere talk: It was meant to encourage action and initative, and to provide students with the tools for both. The firing was a clear provocation and the students responded. As my father put it in his book *The Conscience of a Liberal,* "Lucky for me, there was a student rebellion." Nearly the entire student body—1,500 out of 1,600 students—signed a petition demanding that the decision against my father be reversed. It ended up being a yearlong fight. The strong support my father received from so many on campus and in the community ended up turning the tide.

"David, you find out who your real friends are in tough times like these," he told me.

He had a lot of friends. That was clear. As one student told my father, "Paul, you taught us how to organize, and it was a pleasure to put it into practice for you."

Campus administrators asked outside political science experts to offer an objective determination of my father's value to the campus. The experts sided strongly with him. Soon he went from facing joblessness to being the youngest tenured professor in Carleton history at age twenty-eight. The makeshift office in our basement was no longer filled with cigar smoke.

I START TO GET WHAT
COMMUNITY ORGANIZING IS ALL ABOUT

My father knew me better than I knew myself. He understood my feelings of embarrassment and awkwardness with his insistence on making a stink over injustice. But he also knew that my immediate feelings didn't really matter or mean anything in the long run. He had his eye on a larger

goal: providing an education that would serve me for a lifetime. He wanted me to have a variety of experiences so I
could see for myself why it was essential to get involved—
even when that was difficult, even when it might involve
self-sacrifice, even when it might make me feel awkward or
embarrassed, especially then.

I'm sure plenty of other sons and daughters of professors
have the feeling of every day being a tutorial, a lesson, but
with my father the lessons were anything but dusty or
abstract. We would be in the waiting room of the doctor's
office and one thing would lead to another. Before I knew
it, he would have spotted the representative of a pharma-
ceutical company and begun interrogating him at length as
everyone in the waiting room feigned interest in years-old
issues of *People* magazine.

"Are you pimping for the drug companies?" my father
would ask. "Are you?"

School board meetings were never dull either, not with
my father. And yes, I really did get dragged along, no matter
how loud and anguished my cries of "But Dad!" Even if he
sat there quietly for an hour, you knew that sooner or later
he was going to go off, get up on his feet—finger jabbing in
the air and wild, curly hair shaking with conviction—and
give a passionate discourse about fairness or rights. What
amazed me, what really made an impression, was that even
if he was worked up, he always spoke with respect to everyone, no matter the disagreement. I think that's why, for years
to come, even many who were on the opposite side of political issues—or political races—would end up developing a

strong mutual respect for him, and often a friendship as well. They could see how deeply his convictions went and how steady he was in letting those convictions guide him. Others his age may have come to see their experiences of the 1960s as a time to be forgotten, edited out of their memories, but for my father, what he learned in those years never faded for him in importance.

"Like so many of his generation, he was swept up in the epic battles to desegregate the South and to end the war in Vietnam," Dennis J. McGrath and Dane Smith wrote in the 1995 book *Professor Wellstone Goes to Washington.* "But unlike many of his peers, Wellstone never changed his 1960s view of politics as a struggle for peace, justice, and equality, the downtrodden on one side and entrenched elites on the other. And he held on to 1960s tactics as well: peaceful confrontation and civil disobedience."[3]

My father got involved with organizing people "at the very bottom," as he put it, and found that involvement engrossing and rewarding. At the time, I could not have believed that the lessons my dad passed on to me by bringing me with him out into the community would stay with me my whole life, but they did. We would be driving to a rally or meeting and he would explain to me in a patient, unhurried voice why this was important and why this was the right way to live. He always strived to instill in me a deep impulse to question authority and think for myself. "Don't just go along with the crowd," he'd say. I'd, of course, be bored, sitting there looking out the window, tapping my foot restlessly. We're not equipped as kids to imagine that one afternoon spent tagging along with your father when you could be throwing a football around in the driveway or watching sports on TV would leave so lasting an imprint. *Gunsmoke* this was not.

My father's first great cause had been the welfare recipients in rural Rice County. He was not just helping them organize, he was also interviewing them for his first book, *How the Rural Poor Got Power,* published in June 1978. In a short but enthusiastic review in the *New York Times Book Review,* Doris Grumbach wrote,

Rarely are books about social action written with simple stylistic grace and honesty. Paul Wellstone, a professor of political science at Carleton College in Minnesota, spent two years as an organizer of a grassroots poor-people's organization in Rice County, Minn. Following two years with the Organization for a Better Rice County (OBRC), during which his political action on behalf of the rural poor almost cost him academic tenure, he wrote this impressive book about his experiences.[4]

She goes on to discuss the problems my father and others were fighting to address in Rice County, including the need for welfare rights and reform, food stamps and day care, and transportation for the elderly, concluding:

⸺ ∞ ⸺

In a short preface, the Harvard psychologist Robert Coles points out that social change of the kind sought by OBRC "is a matter of gradual, undramatic, localist transformation—arguably the essence of a democratic process, in contrast to a totalitarian one." Professor Wellstone's book in its persuasive directness may be a landmark in the description of that process.[5]

⸺ ∞ ⸺

His next major fight was standing with farmers in rural Minnesota in opposition to a planned 430-mile power line that would run from coal-burning plants in North Dakota to the Twin Cities, cutting through vast amounts of farmland. Naturally, the large farm conglomerates had the political clout and influence to make sure the proposed line would skirt their holdings, but not so with hundreds of smaller farmers. A farmer named Virgil Fuchs got wind of the plan and encouraged his fellow farmers to organize. And organize and protest they did, but the power line was still built through their properties. Pretty much the only tactic left to them afterward was to become "bolt weevils," as they dubbed themselves, making sure the energy companies would pay a hefty price for running roughshod over their livelihood.

Once again, I remember long drives with my dad as he met with these farmers, him talking through the issues with me before we arrived, maybe thinking aloud in a way, and then sitting in the homes of these small farmers, talking strategy and tactics. They were very creative in their methods. They had bolt weevil T-shirts printed up saying *"weevilus unboltus"* with a picture of a power line tower toppling over. After the line was installed, my dad and I were visiting a farm one day when the cops moved in and the farmers responded by cranking up the manure spreaders to full blast, spraying the cops. That really stayed with me, people chuckling at the dinner table about that. It was a matter of life and death for them, but they could find a way to laugh about it with *weevilus unboltus,* their way of saying "We will unbolt!" They brought down more than a dozen power line towers in the end.

On the ride home, I would ask my dad about all that we had seen and heard. He would look out on the road, his face furrowed with seriousness, and try to convey the depths of this injustice being done and the need to do something about it. These people had spent their whole lives working to make a life, and then some energy companies got the idea to put towers on their land so they could run power to factories in the Twin Cities. It goes back to the lesson that just because it's being done, doesn't make it right.

One of the first political buttons I ever had was one that said "Stop the Power Line." Another I had back then said "Fred Harris for President" in honor of the former Oklahoma senator who drove around in an RV campaigning for the presidency in 1976 to push for what he called "economic democracy." But easily my favorite political button was the one that asked "Who Decides?" My father was very proud.

DAD AND I STAND EYE TO EYE WITH THE NATIONAL GUARD SWINGING BATONS

It was clear my father would have to get involved sooner or later when the Hormel hog processing plant in Austin, Minnesota, announced that it was slashing the hourly wage of its approximately 1,500 meatpackers from $10.69 to $8.25 an hour in late 1984. The company knew a strike was coming— its first in fifty-two years. And come it did. Local P-9 of the United Food and Commercial Workers union voted to strike the following August, and the conflict soon turned ugly. The company threatened to relocate its plant and produce Spam and Wrangler sausages elsewhere, which would have devastated the town of 23,000 in southern Minnesota, a dozen miles from the Iowa border. The town's entire economy depended on Hormel's flagship production plant—and the strike had tensions running very high.

A settlement still had not been reached by the following January, and so Hormel upped the stakes by hiring permanent replacement workers. It was a bitter cold dawn, down around zero degrees, when the first replacement workers showed up to cries of "Scab!" from the hundreds of strikers out front picketing. A week later, when tensions rose even higher and more than one scuffle broke out, Governor Rudy Perpich, who had worked with my dad, decided to send in the National Guard to restore order. Of the 1,500 striking workers, Hormel claimed 70 had applied to return to work— a number no one in the union believed.

My dad brought me down there with him to support the workers, carrying a picket sign the way my father did. Over the previous year, he'd spent a lot of time in Austin with these folks both as they organized for the strike and when they finally walked out. As always, I grumbled as he and I drove down to Austin, but once we arrived I shut up fast. The sense of confrontation hung in the air like the anticipation of a hammer striking an anvil. The meatpackers' situation was not looking good. With a reported eight hundred Guard members mobilized, the striking workers were going to find it difficult to continue their tactic of "fighting from their cars," as they put it, meaning blocking workers from crossing the line.

My dad and I walked around, and everywhere he could, my father shook hands and slapped people on the back, just to pick up their spirits a little and show he stood with them. He was doing his best to pump them up. It was really important for them to see that other people, nonunion members, cared about their struggle. We were out-of-towners, so the fact that we cared enough to come out meant a lot to people. To the day he died, my father continued friendships with men and women who worked at the Hormel plant and in the community based on that connection, because he stood with them then when few others did. It gave them a huge jolt of energy.

I'll never forget the feeling of standing there with the workers as the line of the National Guard approached in full riot gear, with billy clubs and shields, ready to crack down on the strikers. My father was always fearless. He passed that on to me. We stood there with the workers and would have stayed as long as they did, but the workers made the decision to retreat, so retreat we did. My dad had sat with them and strategized for hours. He had shown that he was with them, shoulder to shoulder. Sometimes that's all you can do.

"YOU WANT TO DO *WHAT* NOW, DAD?"

When my dad told me in 1989 he planned to run for the U.S. Senate in the next year's election, my first reaction was to laugh.

"You're kidding me," I said. "What are you *doing?* This is embarrassing. You're a college teacher, not a politician. You don't talk like them and you don't act like them."

"Exactly," he said.

Keep in mind, my father had run for office before. He'd done great, too, had shown a real flair for giving eloquent, powerful speeches that could move people and also get them to think. He was good at campaigning. He had a knack for getting up early and shaking hands with every last person drinking coffee down at the café on Main Street, and the rallies and barbecues, the strategy and teamwork. The problem with that first foray in 1982 was that he'd been singularly unqualified for the office he was seeking, that of state auditor—a position that amounted to keeping the books for the state. An accountant he was not. Even he understood that. But he got the odd idea to run and base his campaign on his support for a nuclear freeze initative. I'm serious. That was his pitch. I was embarrassed back then, too, and would love to have avoided getting dressed up and posing for family pictures, passing out flyers, and generally putting ourselves out there during the campaign, but no such luck.

Now, eight years later, he wanted to run for the United States Senate against an incumbent, Rudy Boschwitz, who had a big war chest and would be very hard to beat. It seemed pointless to me. Dad was going to lose. People were going to take shots at him. We were all going to feel very frustrated. But I'd spent my life watching my father in action at school board meetings and protest rallies and organizing sessions, so I knew once he got going on something, there was no stopping him. He knew this was a good chance to bring forth certain issues and make a statement that people with actual political convictions could run for office. Inexperience didn't have to be a disqualification.

I tried to stay out of it as much as I could, which was not hard since by then I was off on my own. I was married and living on a farm about an hour south of my parents' home, and working as a corrections officer in Rochester, Minnesota. I liked it. The first week there, some of the inmates tried to intimidate me. They didn't know I was a former wrestler. They just saw that I was a little guy. So I got right in their faces, showed no fear, and didn't back down. They never messed with me again after that.

I bought an organic farm in Chatfield right on the Root River, which flows into the Upper Mississippi, and was working long hours getting that set up along with my wife, Tammy. It was a good ninety miles from my home up to the Twin Cities, so I did not have much to do with my father's whirlwind first run for the Senate. He and I talked at least once a week and he would tell me what was going on. If he was doing a parade or barbecue down near me in southern Minnesota, then I would come out for that or he would come see me on the farm, a place he loved. Dad loved campaigning because he was doing what mattered to him most, talking about getting involved and staying involved, offering the kinds of lessons in life he had been offering me all those times I rode shotgun with him to help this or that group organize. Now he had a wider audience and they were listening.

It says a lot about what a long shot my father was in that 1990 race that the national press completely overlooked him until he stunned the political establishment by taking 60 percent of the vote in the Democratic primary to just 35 percent for Jim Nichols, the state agriculture commissioner. Even then, the New York Times dismissed him with a few words: "The incumbent Senator, Rudy Boschwitz, a Republican, easily won renomination and will face Paul Wellstone, a political science professor."[6]

To political reporters, dismissing an unknown candidate with as curt a description as "a political science professor" meant about as much as a high school student summing up her potential prom date as "a really sweet guy." The East Coast elite political media thought my father had no chance, so they ignored him.

The truth was, my father didn't think he had any shot against Boschwitz. He was outspent by more than six to one, yet he was also more clever than his opponent. The best campaign ad was that famous "Fast Paul" commercial where my father explained, "Unlike my opponent, I don't have six million dollars, so I'm gonna have to talk fast" and went through a rapid-fire introduction of himself, his family, his background, and his message. It was his sly way of making fun of himself and making fun of traditional politics, but it totally worked. People loved it and the TV stations kept replaying it on their news broadcasts. If you walked anywhere in the state, you'd hear people making comments about that spot, a surefire sign that something was happening. My dad's campaign took on a life of its own. Lightning struck.

"No one ever expected us to get this close, David," he told me a week before Election Day.

He was resigned to losing, however. He'd closed the gap to a few percentage points in the polls, but the experts were all still picking Boschwitz. My father was looking ahead to running for the Senate the next time.

"We'll get real close and then the next time, we'll win," he told me then.

My dad went to bed on the night before Election Day believing in that prediction—and of course I did, too. But as it turned out, my family figured in the final outcome in a way that no one could have predicted. Seeing his lead narrow, Boschwitz got scared and lashed out with some highly unfortunate remarks, attacking my father as a so-called bad Jew because he married outside the faith and didn't give my brother and sister and me a religious upbringing. It was a blunt and ugly attempt by Boschwitz, who was also Jewish, to pull some Christian votes loose. Instead, it backfired. My father came right back at Boschwitz, saying, "He has a problem with Christians, then," and Minnesota TV did the rest, repeating the clip over and over. My father pulled out a narrow victory, one of the great upsets in Senate history, all made possible by the huge numbers of volunteers and activists who mobilized on behalf of him and his populist message during that campaign.

"I will work so hard to live up to your trust," my father declared on the night he was elected, and he spent the next twelve years in the Senate trying to follow through on those words and to join the proud fighting progressive Minnesota tradition of such major figures as Hubert Humphrey, Eugene McCarthy, and Walter Mondale. "I will work so hard to do well by you. I will work so hard to be a senator that you will be proud of."

CHAPTER 3

LOSING MY ADVISOR
AND MY SUPPORT NETWORK

*W*alter Mondale was waiting on me. The former vice president and favorite son of Minnesota needed to hear from me, but I wasn't ready. My father was gone, and so were my mother and my sister. Everything was a blur. There were important decisions to be made and I was the one who needed to make them. No one expected me and my brother to play kingmaker. We were not the ones doing the heavy lifting on deciding who would run in my father's place for the Senate. This was not a Mel Carnahan–type situation. Melvin Carnahan was Missouri's governor who was running for the U.S. Senate when he died in a plane crash three weeks before the 2000 election. Missouri law would not allow his name to be removed from the ballot and he was posthumously elected. Upon Carnahan's death, the lieutenant governor became governor and appointed Carnahan's wife to the Senate seat until a special election could be held in November 2002. State law in Minnesota was different. It called for my father's name to be stricken from the ballot and for another to be added as the candidate for the Democratic party. With the crash only eleven days before the election, this would be a tall order. I knew Mondale was an excellent choice, an honorable man my father admired and knew well, but I was having so much trouble getting a handle on all that had happened. I was going on autopilot. It all seemed mechanical. I could not seem to break out of that.

I needed my best advisor. I needed my father. My whole life, he was the one I had turned to when I needed a dose of good judgment and tough love. He was not only wickedly smart and generous with his understanding and insight, but incapable of sugarcoating anything or mincing words. Until now, I had always had that clear, passionate, commanding voice at the ready to give me a nudge when I needed one, or just to hear me out. It was just too much for me to process that he was gone. I couldn't believe it. I felt like it was all some kind of horrible trick being played, and if I could only figure it out, I could call him somehow, or see him, and he'd be there advising me again.

I would call my parents' house, knowing full well they were not going to answer, but wanting to hear my mother's voice on the answering machine. The shock over not having my father there hurt and saddened me, and made me want to turn to the emotional support and adviser I'd always looked to in an emergency: my mother. I'm not just talking about the steady presence in my life all those years, when she would make me lunch and we would talk over my day, but the way she had of understanding just what I was saying—or not saying—and probing for answers, but always gently, so I never felt interrogated but came away understanding my own feelings and thoughts much better. Mom had a knack for knowing when you needed her. She always knew by intuition when something was going on and would show up at just the right time, even without a phone call.

My mother went through a kind of transformation following my father's political rise. She had resisted speaking in public as long as she could, but once she got out there she wowed people with her style. Even more so, it was the little things. She would go in and meet with children staying at a battered women's shelter, not just to say hello, but to look at their artwork with them and listen to them and make them feel special. She was always very good at adding a personal touch. But in her own way she was every bit as much a fighter as my father. As I said at the memorial on the University of Minnesota campus, "My mom was everything to us. My dad wasn't who he was without my mom."

Everything was so confusing. My father's political team was handling everything, but they still needed me, as my father's son, to give my blessing with the replacement campaign. They needed me there at the meeting with former Vice President Mondale to put into words what my father would have wanted. Fritz had not decided what he was going to do at this point. Before he saw us, he'd received phone calls from two senators, Pat Leahy and Ted Kennedy, urging him to run. He'd also been called by Majority Leader Tom Daschle, promising him a position in the Senate leadership if he was elected. Jeff Blodgett, my father's campaign manager, had made it clear that the Wellstone campaign operation, headed up by Jeff himself, would be geared up behind Mondale at full blast.

The meeting was at the downtown Minneapolis offices of Dorsey and Whitney, Mondale's law firm, at ten that Saturday morning, the day after the crash and three days before the planned memorial service at the University of Minnesota. Jeff Blodgett and Rick Kahn were also attending the meeting. I don't even know if it's right to say I was nervous. It's hard to describe. It felt like I was just out of it, as if I were watching myself in the middle of some movie endlessly spooling forward, words coming out of my mouth, without ever having noticed that I planned to speak.

Mondale was in the lobby to greet us, wearing a comfortable-looking pair of khakis and a sweater. He walked up to me and gave me a big hug right away and was very emotional as he gave his condolences for my loss. We followed him back to the office, which I remember being very empty, and just to loosen up the somber mood a little, he started pulling plastic water bottles out of his little office refrigerator and tossing them to each of us. I caught mine and was relieved. In the state I was in I thought it might go right past me.

"Thank you for seeing us, Mr. Vice President," I said to start the meeting. "I'm sure both my parents would want you to be the one to carry on my father's work in the Senate."

I mentioned in particular how Mondale's emphasis on education and health care, especially mental health issues, lined up well with my father's interest in those issues and was something they had in common as senators.

Mondale laughed about the way my father had come to Washington, so full of vinegar that he ticked off half the city within the first month, but then soon learned from his mistakes and turned himself into a highly regarded legislator who was very able to work within the system. That was the kind of growth Mondale admired, he said. He respected the way my father built relationships with senators, both Democrats and Republicans.

"I don't know that I've ever seen anyone who could fire up a crowd the way your father could," he said during our meeting.

Mondale did turn serious at one point in a way I would not have expected, but immediately respected. He said he did have one difference of opinion with my father, and that concerned the pledge my father had made when he first ran for Senate that he would limit himself to two terms. Mondale felt that it had not been wise to retract that pledge and run for a third term in 2002. He added quickly that he did not want to talk in detail about politics, since it was a time for mourning, but he was very gracious in thanking us for coming.

Forty-five minutes after it started, the meeting was over and I could exhale. You do your best just to get through times like that. But at least the meeting achieved the desired result. Mondale had heard all he needed—though the world wouldn't know that just yet.

Eric Black reported the meeting in the next morning's *Minneapolis Star Tribune:*

———<small>⚮</small>———

U.S. Sen. Paul Wellstone's eldest son, his campaign manager and an old friend implored Walter Mondale at an emotional meeting Saturday morning to take Wellstone's place on the November ballot, and Mondale is highly likely to make the run, according to one of those present at the meeting. The former vice president and U.S. senator did not commit himself, saying that he would not comment publicly on his plans until after Tuesday evening's memorial service for Wellstone, the person at the meeting said. . . .

Speculation has run rampant in political circles, with most analysts agreeing that Mondale would be the party's strongest candidate, if he is willing to come out of political retirement at age 74. He has been bombarded with calls and e-mails from longtime friends and allies urging him to step forward.

But Wellstone's son and closest political associates had not made their wishes known until the meeting Saturday at the office of Mondale's law firm.[7]

———<small>⚮</small>———

Here is how Mondale later described the encounter in his own book, *The Good Fight: A Life in Liberal Politics.*

———∞∞∞———

Jeff Blodgett arrived with David Wellstone, Paul's son, and Rick Kahn, a close friend of Paul's and his campaign treasurer. His eyes red with grief, David Wellstone made a personal request that I enter the race. He was crestfallen that his father's voice would be silenced, and he conveyed the family's view that I was the only candidate who had a chance to hold the seat. . . . I knew there was no time for equivocation, and by the time we finished, I had made up my mind. I had the elements I needed: a unified party behind me, a personal request from the Wellstone family, and the Wellstone campaign operation waiting to go. I said yes.[8]

———∞∞∞———

THE MEMORIAL SERVICE

We knew there was never going to be a way to make everyone happy or satisfy everyone's expectations in memorializing my father and mother and sister and the five others who died in the crash. We decided to hold the memorial in Williams Arena at the U of M campus, where my father and I had enjoyed watching many a wrestling match together. The White House sent word that Vice President Cheney would like to attend, but we talked it over and agreed that the incredible security measures in place at that time, barely a year after the September 11 attacks, made it a bad idea for the vice president to attend. But many other Republicans did, including Norm Coleman, who up until a week before was out on the campaign stump telling the people of Minnesota why they should vote for him for Senate and not my dad.

It was a beautiful, moving memorial. One of my favorite parts was the video montage of my father set to "Forever Young" by Bob Dylan, my father's inspiration in so many ways. "Politics is not about winning for the sake of winning," my father said in a video clip played at the service. "Politics is about the improvement of people's lives."

I was a nervous wreck, having to speak in front of so many people. I felt a great weight of responsibility to rise to the occasion and speak with calm and dignity and do right by my father, my mother, and my sister. I talked about sitting on his lap when I was a kid and how he would let me drive up the driveway. I talked about how my mother would whip up a smorgasbord of food in the kitchen to try and keep everyone happy. I talked about my sister and how the same iron will that ran in the family showed up in her in a way that led her to run marathons. I talked about the need to carry on, looking beyond the crash, beyond that numb, confused week of mourning, beyond the election coming up in one week. I talked of the need to heed the lessons of my father's example for as long as that memory remained alive and always to look for a way to help other people.

Only later did I come to understand how the power of a few isolated clips and slanted commentary gave people a completely inaccurate impression of the memorial. The problem with spin is there is no answering it. A false story was presented to the country of my father's memorial as some kind of extreme display of partisan zeal as opposed to what it was— a memorial and a call to live my father's principles, which were, above all, to keep fighting for the disadvantaged. That's not a partisan message. That should be a priority for all. But once the spin got going, it influenced a lot of people. For example, the *New York Times* described the memorial in this way: "Some 20,000 people, including Bill Clinton, Al Gore and the Rev. Jesse Jackson, packed into two sports stadiums in Minneapolis for a somber memorial to Paul Wellstone." That article referred readers to page A23, where they found a highly opinionated headline: "Memorial for Wellstone Assumes Spirit of Rally." What happened to "somber"?

In the category of questionable taste, one commentator wrote an entire column in a national newspaper as if she were inside my father's head and knew what he would have thought about the memorial. I am not going to deny that when I first saw that, I was outraged. How about a little respect for the dead? But my anger has long since cooled. It was an election season, and there are always going to be people with no compunctions about using events like that in whatever way they see fit to try and push a particular viewpoint. That is politics. Getting angry does not help the situation. It only helps those who seek to manipulate others. I try not to engage in that. I want to engage in the politics of healing.

In fact, I hope one day to write another book on the subject of healing in politics. I'd like to talk about the lessons I've learned, and lessons we should all learn. The first is that hate in politics is radioactive. It's like toxic waste that pollutes the environment, not just for an hour, not just for a day, but for years, even generations. I have no time to spew hate at anyone. I have no stomach for that. It doesn't help anyone. We all know this on some deep level, but nevertheless something is in the air that has people addled and grumpy and quick to lash out at others. Is the rapid pace of technological change to blame for the uglier mood of our politics? Or shifts in what we expect out of our economic futures and the insecurity that breeds? These and a hundred other trends all working in uneasy unison? It really doesn't matter. The point is: Change starts now, and change starts within. True, lasting change comes when we live our values day in and day out and put them into action.

I KEEP THINKING BACK ON MY FATHER'S LIMP

If I could just skip the months after the death of my parents and sister, that would be my first choice. I'd prefer to avoid reliving it all again, those first few months, really those first few years after the crash. My memories are too vivid, in that way that nothing is as vivid as a fresh jolt of pain, and too cloudy and confusing. During that period, my father was more present than ever in my life, every minute of every day, even as my vision of him went through a confusing series of shifts. In some ways, I felt I could see him more clearly and understand him better than I ever had when he was alive.

I found myself thinking often of my father's limp. Through most of his life, he would have been the last person you'd think would walk with any sort of limp. He was a wrestler and a runner, an athlete, a very fit man with a burly chest and a bounce in his step. He was energy and physical ease personified. He felt comfortable in his skin and moved well. That was why it hit us all like a thunderbolt when he started having problems walking. Not many people know this, but in his late thirties he developed a form of multiple sclerosis, which was not diagnosed until January 2002, earlier in the year he died. He was lucky. It was a limited form of MS that would not have been life threatening, though it did give him problems. He quietly made a low-key public announcement of the diagnosis that final year, soon after it emerged, but up until then we never knew.

His leg would kind of kick out to the side when he walked. It looked odd, I freely admit that. We would be out in public and he would get some strange looks. I felt very protective of him. I remember going to a Vikings game with him, and him finding those little concrete steps very difficult, with no rail or handhold, nearly tripping with every step. People recognized my father wherever he went by then, of course.

"Hey look—he's almost tripping!" some guy called out loud so everyone could hear. "Senator Wellstone is drunk!"

I wanted to deck the guy who said that, but kept myself under control. We didn't know at the time about my dad's MS. He had this weird pain in his neck and kept going to doctors for years, but none of them ever diagnosed it as MS. It was a mystery. He crashed his bike one day on a casual ride. He wiped out, people saw him, and you knew they talked about that, too—a U.S. senator falling down on the side of the road. I'm sure that started some rumors. I didn't know what to say to him after that. You just kind of shake your head and say, "What are you doing?"

Then came the diagnosis. MS is a highly heritable disease, so that means your chances of contracting the disease of the nervous system go way up. It can freak you out—with every leg twitch, the thought crosses your mind and you think, "Could this be it?"

We didn't have time to digest any of that when he was alive. Not until my father was gone did it really sink in what pain he must have quietly endured and how difficult it must have been for him, this energetic, athletic man, to accept a sense of physical limitation. It was, in a way, a glimpse of mortality. He could have been slowed down by it, but he never was. He refused to change anything he did. He was going to confront his own mortality, his own ultimate decline, and put as much determination and energy into that struggle as he had put into organizing for other people's struggles all those years.

SORTING THROUGH EVERYONE ELSE'S VIEWS OF MY FATHER

As I mentioned earlier, it was a bizarre situation for me in Minnesota during those first few months after the crash. So many people felt they had lost a friend when my father died, even people who had never met him but felt as if they had. I wanted to be as respectful and considerate as possible every time someone approached me to try and explain what my father meant to them, how his example of fighting for what's right had resonated, or how some specific effort or position of my father's had been especially meaningful to this person standing in front of me. I wanted to be as courteous as I could because that was the right thing to do—and my father had instilled in me the value of doing the right thing even when that meant overcoming the distractions and challenges of life—and also because I felt it was one way I could honor the memory of my father, mother, and sister.

But it got harder and harder to handle the challenge of being there for other people. If I brushed people off and tried to get away at the supermarket or a pizza joint, picking up a large pepperoni to go, then I felt bad. I felt like I was being churlish. But if I went out of my way to hear out what people wanted to tell me, I soon found it could be a hazardous experience. It wasn't just the time it took. Once people started, they had a lot to say. My pizza would be cold and congealing, and still they would talk, eyes imploring me to understand. Often they would want me to give them a hug, to buck them up, to make them feel better. This I often did. I wanted people to feel better. But it got to be more and more difficult. How could I comfort other people when I had no way to comfort myself?

I didn't even know how to think of my father anymore. He and I had been so close and had shared so much, he was like a great friend whose presence was constant, to the point where I knew what he would think on just about any point and so, in a way, could consult him without even doing so. I would recall the times I rode shotgun with him on the drive out to see those farmers, sitting around their kitchen tables and eating little crustless sandwiches and lemonade, or beer all around, organizing a response to the giant power line being planned to rip right through their farmland. I would remember standing side by side with my father and dozens of union workers at that Hormel hog-processing plant in Austin, Minnesota, forming a line of solidarity as the National Guard members waved their batons in the air and closed in, riot shields and grim looks both locked in place. I would think of the rides home after these and so many other learning experiences and the talks we would have, my father calmly and patiently explaining once again why it was important to get involved and fight for the powerless. Or I would think of going for long runs with my father, or playing two-on-two with the neighbor kids in front of our house on the street with the Catholic church down at one end.

But the more I heard from other people about their idea of who Paul Wellstone was and what he meant, the more it felt like I was losing something, the more it felt like my very personal, very internal version of my dad was being stolen from me. I hated this feeling, but sensed there was nothing I could do about it. Weeks passed after the crash and it only got worse. Months passed and still I was always being pulled in the direction of seeing my father through the eyes of others, all the more so when people singled him out for praise and admiration.

The December after the crash, *Time* magazine came out with its annual "Person of the Year" issue and my father was included among the Persons of the Year. Harriet Barovick wrote a nice little article titled "Washington's Latter Day Mr. Smith":

—⊷∞⊶—

*It's easy to picture Paul Wellstone's life as a Hollywood
movie: scrappy unknown idealist, married to his high
school sweetheart, overcomes solid incumbent to win
a seat in the Senate. There he storms, and eventually
charms, Washington with his rabble-rousing advocacy
for the downtrodden. Before he was killed in a plane
crash just days before the November election, the
Minnesotan son of Russian-Jewish immigrants was
a voice for laborers, the poor and the mentally ill,
emphatically embracing the long-out-of-fashion label
"liberal." In October, Wellstone was one of 23 Senators
to vote against the resolution to authorize using force
against Iraq. His righteous indignation and occasionally
long-winded speeches could grate, but he won respect
and personal affection on both sides of the aisle for
that rare trait in Washington: staying true to himself,
no matter the political risk.*[9]

—⊷∞⊶—

Most of the tributes to my father came from people in
Minnesota, of course, where the loss was felt much more
deeply and where the stories of his various causes and
fights hit much closer to home. Often it was the former
Minnesotans, people like Bob Dylan who had been raised
there but then moved away, who were the most likely to
muse over my father's death and what it meant.

Some of the most moving tributes were from people who
wrote into the National Organization for Women to honor

the memories of both my parents. Pamela Moos in Topanga, California, wrote one that stood out in particular:

—∽∾∽—

I have heard of deaths of other "famous" people, like Princess Di, but they did not affect me this deeply. I have shed a tear on more than one occasion thinking out the loss of these great people. I think this comes from my close connection with Paul and Sheila Wellstone.

I voted for him twice before I left Minnesota, where I was born and raised. I met him several times while in school on field trips or at political functions or rallies. Both he and Sheila always took time to speak with you and always made me feel comfortable and confident talking with them. Each time I felt like I was really being heard.

Even though I have left the state, it has never left my heart. I will always be a Minnesota girl and when I vote here in California this year, I will again shed a tear that I will not be able to vote for Wellstone this year.

Sheila and Paul, you did so much for us and we are grateful. I have personally been affected by the good you have done in Washington and will always be glad for your presence there. My only condolence is that you are together. I hope that no matter where you have gone, you are able to continue doing good because that is what you were born to do.

May your souls have peace and may someone with your passion step up and take your place. Thank you

*for all your years of service. They have been noted and
very appreciated.*

  Love always, Pamela Moos.[10]

These and many, many other warm tributes echoed in my
thoughts. I am thankful to everyone who honored my father,
and especially to those who also honored my mother and my
sister. I would not have wanted their deaths to be marked in
silence. I would not have wanted to have had the sense, a
week or a month after the crash, that everyone had already
forgotten about them. It's good to have the people we love
remembered. But it also created a problem for me. With all
these words ringing in my ears, all these tributes, how was I
ever going to return to my own thoughts, my own words,
and my own private tribute to my father and my mother and
my sister?

I kept thinking about a conversation my father and I had
the month he died about the importance of following your
moral compass, of always doing your best to do what's right,
at whatever cost to yourself. My father had voted in 1991
against authorizing the Gulf War against Iraq and now, in
October 2002, a close vote was coming up on whether to
authorize President George W. Bush to pursue a war against
Saddam Hussein. My dad was in a tough fight for re-election,
with many in Minnesota in favor of the war. He was the only
senator up for re-election who opposed the Iraq War, and one
of only eleven in the Senate who would vote against both the
Persian Gulf War and the Iraq War.

As Helen Dewar explained the situation in the *Washington Post* on October 9 of that year, "Anti-war activists were conducting a three-day sit-in at his St. Paul office, even as his Republican challenger was pummeling him as wobbly on national security. For Sen. Paul D. Wellstone (D-Minn.), the Iraq war resolution before Congress presented a lose-lose proposition likely to anger voters he needs in his tight re-election bid. But to Wellstone there was never really much of a choice."

He had me over one Sunday before the vote to tell me about what was coming. He'd gotten up early at five o'clock in the morning, as he always did, to sit down with a pile of Sunday newspapers and read them all, starting with the local papers, the *St. Paul Pioneer Press* and the *Minneapolis Star Tribune,* and then working up to the Sunday *New York Times.* We ate a breakfast together of waffles and bacon, my mom upstairs, just my dad and I alone at the table.

He was in a somber mood. A part of him would have been relieved if he could be persuaded that, as much as he hated war, this war was both inevitable and just. He was human, after all. He hated the idea of losing and no longer being able to use the platform he had gained to work for change. The political pros were all telling him, "You can't do this! It's political suicide to vote against this war!" But he just could not find a rationale that made any sense to him.

"I just don't believe this war is right, David," he told me. "I haven't seen proof that Saddam really has these weapons of mass destruction we keep hearing about."

Of course he hadn't. No one had seen that proof—because there wasn't any.

"I'm going to oppose this war, David, and I want you to understand that I probably will lose my Senate seat because of it. I'm going to be called unpatriotic. I'm going to be called a lot worse. It's not going to be easy, not for anyone in the family."

"As if it's ever easy for us!" I said, kidding my dad a little. "You have to do what you think is right. That's who you are. That's who you've always been."

A part of me wanted to ask him some tougher questions. I knew he was right when it came to the argument for war, but I also knew the air was filled with a kind of war fever, an emotional lust for national action, and in a way it seemed perverse of him to provoke the wave of criticism he would have coming. A part of me wanted to say, "Jeez, Dad, do you *have* to do this?" But I knew that would have been pointless. I knew my father always felt driven to follow the truth and to do what was right.

His continuing legacy springs from his absolute integrity and his refusal to let Washington change him. He never let the power and the money and the whole scene inside the Beltway influence who he was or how he went about his business. Although he was now called "Senator" and looked a little different in a suit, it never changed him. He was still fundamentally the same person who used to sit down with mothers on welfare and farmers and stand up at countless school board meetings, even as he spoke out against injustice during a Senate committee meeting in Washington. It was all the same to him. He was always the same, just on a different stage. That to me was the part of his legacy that I would always work hardest to uphold and represent in my own life.

WATCH OUT FOR THE EAGLES

he bald eagles pointed me forward, even though I didn't know it at first. You often do not understand as you muddle through a difficult situation just what to make of the clues you pick up to help you find the right direction, which ones hit you at the time, but then float away from your consciousness, and which end up linking together with other events to offer a clear theme. I knew enough in those walking-blind days and weeks after the crash to understand that it might be a long, long time before I felt like I had my life back again, if I would ever feel that way again. But at the same time, it's only human and natural to start looking for immediate answers. The eagles were there for me. They kept me company. At first they just seemed beautiful and spiritual and strong, distant but also very present. Eventually, I realized they had a more specific message for me that I would only come to understand with time.

If I said that catching my first glimpse of a group of bald eagles in Minnesota made me think of the Romantic poet William Blake, you'd think I was trying to put one over on you, but later, when I started looking into eagles and what they have meant to people, I came across this quote from Blake that gets across some of what I felt about eagles the year after the crash . . . and still feel.

"When thou seest an eagle, thou seest a portion of genius. Lift up thy head," Blake wrote in a poem he called "The Marriage of Heaven and Hell."

The first day after the crash was, in some ways, the worst. We were not allowed back to the spot near the Minnesota Iron Range where the plane had gone down that day because the Federation Aviation Administration (FAA) and National Transportation Safety Board (NTSB) were flooding the area with investigators to search for any small clues that could explain the crash. After all, my father had flown repeatedly in this same little plane during the campaign without an incident, and it was only a forty-minute flight. A lot of people suspected foul play, an idea that only picked up momentum when the FAA announced what was described as a "slight irregularity" with the radio beacon at the little airport in Eveleth where the plane was scheduled to land. Investigators were searching by hand through the debris in the woods a couple of miles away from the airport where the plane crashed. They found a gauge from the control panel and took that away for analysis. I didn't have time for conspiracy theories then, and I don't have time for them now. It was an accident, what happened, a very unfortunate accident—not the result of a sinister plot cooked up by some nefarious political element.

On the second day after the crash, my brother and I were allowed to head up to the crash site along with the family members of the others who had died. They loaded us all on a bus at a staging area a few miles from the crash site, and as soon as I found a window seat in the middle of the bus and looked out I could see bald eagles following us. My brother, Mark, and I did not talk a lot on that drive, just sat together and looked out the windows watching the eagles. There was so much to say and so much not to say. We'd been a close-knit family of five two days earlier and now it was just me and my kid brother, seven years younger than me. We would have to be brothers to each other, but also father and son and son and father.

When we arrived at the site, we were faced with an eerie scene. Scraps of charred metal were littered here and there. The smell of jet fuel lingered. The area was swampy in places and wooded in others. I wandered around, and that is when I found the flower and left it for my father, sure he could not be gone. This all had to be some kind of big misunderstanding. He and my mother and my sister were going to appear any minute and life would go on. But the woods up there in the Iron Range were so quiet, so isolated, the chances of that happening did feel awfully remote. But still, I hoped. And still, I hated to leave. They called us back to the bus to take us away, but I lingered. I didn't want to go. Finally, I climbed up the steps and took a seat, then stared out the window as the bus lurched into gear and pulled away.

As the bus drove away, I saw three bald eagles nesting in the trees near the crash site. My brother saw them, too. If you've never watched bald eagles flying over you, it's hard to convey how strong a presence they have. Some Native Americans believe that bald eagles can fly back and forth between our world and the spirit world, that they are sacred messengers. Others believe they are ancestral spirits. My brother and I saw those amazing birds up there and had a strong feeling of just why Native Americans see these birds as unique and special. There were three eagles, one each for my sister, my mother, and my father. Mark and I felt a strong connection to our parents and sister through those birds, and the feeling only grew stronger as the bus continued on and the trio of bald eagles kept following to keep an eye on us from up above.

I was starting to get a sense of why our Founding Fathers had taken such a shine to bald eagles. That's why we have a bald eagle on the Great Seal of the United States, as it's called, first designed back in 1782. We see it to this day on the presidential seal, which features a bald eagle in profile at the center of the image. The associations then were with strength and autonomy, the ability to go one's own way. As *Time* magazine wrote in a 1935 article about the birds, "The bald eagle is handsome, majestic, tremendously powerful. An individualist, it is rarely seen in the company of more than one of its kind. These attributes make U.S. citizens unversed in Nature proud to acknowledge the bald eagle as their national bird and emblem."

But that was in 1935. A lot had changed with our national bird over the decades since then. By 1976, the Associated Press reported, "After 200 years of nationhood, the United States now may be forced to list its national symbol, the bald eagle, as an endangered species—a victim of shooting, pesticides and human intrusion."

By the time my father got to the Senate, the bald eagle was making a comeback—and I remember how excited he was in November 1991 when he was asked to release a bald eagle into the wild that had been rehabilitated. According to a report that year from the University of Minnesota Raptor Center, the birds, which can have wingspans of up to eight feet, only develop the famous white head and tail when they are four to five years of age. Before that, they are dark brown. The report explained: "Formerly distributed across North America, they are now limited to breeding in Alaska, Canada, the northern Great Lakes states, Florida, and the Pacific Northwest. In Minnesota, they commonly breed on northern lakes and along the St. Croix and Mississippi Rivers. Bald eagles move south for the winter to open water areas that attract large numbers of waterfowl or fish. In Minnesota, this includes the Minnesota and Mississippi Rivers and sometimes lakes in the southern part of the state."

The Raptor Center had cared for and rehabilitated the two bald eagles that were ready to be released that Veterans Day. I still have a picture of my father, showing how excited he was to hold an eagle aloft and release it. I thought of that day and that picture when I saw those eagles following the bus that was taking us away from the crash site. Three weeks after the crash, the Raptor Center contacted my brother and me to tell us they had another eagle to release. This time, I had the privilege of tossing the majestic bird from my arms and watching it soar away with three mighty flaps of its wings, just as my father had earlier.

THE EAGLES MAKE AN APPEARANCE
AT THE MEMORIAL

I never really wrote a speech to read at the memorial for my parents, sister, and campaign aides held at the University of Minnesota in front of more than 20,000 people and broadcast on national television. Every day passed in such a blur, I never had time for that. I just jotted down some notes to guide myself as well as I could and then went up there and spoke from the heart. I knew I was going to close my remarks with a reference to those eagles, but it wasn't until I was actually speaking at the memorial that the exact words came to me.

I recalled a time not long before when my father had come back from a visit to the Red Lake Indian Reservation. "I was getting ready to speak," my father had explained to me. "And just as I got up there, the spiritual leader came up to me and said, 'The eagle passed by as you were up there. That's a very good sign.'"

I then told the story of going up to the crash site and seeing what looked like a huge, white ball on the road that flew up into a tree and perched there.

"As we went by, we looked and it was a huge bald eagle perched there looking out over us," I said at the gathering. "Make of it what you want, but I'll tell you what I think: I think that my father, my mother, my sister, and all the others, are there looking over us. Thank you for coming. Thank you for loving my father."

I knew my talk had resonated with a lot of people, especially the closing, but I was still amazed to realize just how deeply it had affected people. As an example of that, let me turn to the words of one of my father's good friends in the Senate, Tom Daschle, who represented South Dakota, a state that shares a lot more with Minnesota than just a border. Here was how Daschle described hearing the news of the crash as he drove with his wife to the Crow Creek Indian Reservation in South Dakota in his book *Like No Other Time: The 107th Congress and the Two Years That Changed America.*

—⊸∞⊶—

At one point early on during that drive, my cell phone service connected and a call came through from my son, Nathan. . . . .

The connection was terrible. I could hardly make out his words. We were cut off a couple of times, but he kept calling back, and we were able to talk a little bit. He asked how I was doing. He'd heard the news and he wanted to make sure I was all right.

That's where it all broke through. I'd kept the grief inside up until then, but this was my son talking to me, my own flesh and blood, and now it just let itself out. I

*broke down and cried—cried as I hadn't done in I don't
know how long.*

*I've driven over a lot of long, lonely stretches of
South Dakota, but that day was the longest, loneliest
drive I think I've ever had. . . . At one point, I looked
off into the distance and saw a bald eagle sitting on
the leafless branch of a tree. The eagle is a powerful
symbol in the Sioux culture, and it's not that common
a sight anymore, not even in such remote parts of this
historically Indian land.*

*I remember being struck enough by the sight of that
eagle that I pointed it out to my security detail. . . . It
would not be until four days later, at Paul's memorial
service, when his son David closed his heart-wrenching
remarks with the story of seeing an eagle drifting above
his dad's crash site, that I was jolted by the powerful
sense of meaning in this moment, of some kind of
connection to Paul.[11]*

⸝⸝⸝

MY BROTHER AND I TRY TO GET AWAY,
BUT THE EAGLES FOLLOW US

Mark and I knew we needed to get away, just the two of us,
and early that winter we got a chance. We decided to drive
to Montana for a ski vacation. We wanted the time together,
just the two of us, to talk or not talk, but most important to
be together as a family. We also both wanted a break from the
craziness and pressure of being a Wellstone in Minnesota in
those months when so many people in the state were reeling

from the plane crash, still deep in shock and confusion and sadness. We wanted time to focus on our own shock and confusion and sadness. So my brother and I loaded up the car and left Minnesota, passing through South Dakota on our way to Montana, and there on the side of the road we saw two bald eagles looking at us. One of them might have been the same eagle that Tom Daschle had spotted in South Dakota only a couple of months earlier, I don't know.

Throughout that trip, I had the feeling that the bald eagles were keeping an eye on us. It was December, a time for family, and we had a place for five days so near the ski slopes we could ski right up to it after a day of kicking up powder. It was a treat for ourselves and it helped keep the bond between us strong. We kept talking on that ski trip about doing something for just the two of us to remind ourselves that even if life might push or pull us each in a different direction in the future, we were still forever connected, not just as brothers who had grown up playing football and hockey on our quiet street in Minnesota, but also as two men who had to live through this horrible, wrenching experience together.

Finally, we realized the eagle was the key. Mark and I got matching tattoos on our right shoulders. The image that we decided would convey all that needed to be said was a bald eagle, along with three feathers—one representing our father, one our mother, and one our sister—set inside a Native American medicine wheel with clouds in the background.

THE EAGLE STILL FOLLOWED ME

A few months after the crash, I received a letter one day out of the blue. I opened it up and a handful of photographs fell out. A woman who lived near the crash site had heard me speak at the memorial service about the bald eagles living near the crash site. She knew those eagles. She lived nearby and was very familiar with them. She had taken some pictures of those same eagles I had seen flying alongside the bus and sent them to me along with a short letter. It was a very generous act that I will never forget.

I have kept those pictures with me ever since. I often pull them out and feel bolstered both to remember my parents and sister but also to move on. I've been to the memorial site many times, and whenever I am back there I think maybe there's a way to meet that woman who sent the pictures and thank her for the remarkable gift she gave me, but I don't have her contact information. If you are out there now, kind stranger, reading these words or hearing me talk about this book, let me say: *Thank you so much. The pictures are beautiful and have sustained me for years. Please get in touch!*

Like a lot of kids who grew up on TV, I tend to think in references to my favorite programs. One I used to enjoy watching with my parents was *Northern Exposure,* that offbeat show set in Alaska, which once included this description of the eagle:

The Eagle wasn't always the Eagle. The Eagle, before he became the Eagle, was Yucatangee, the Talker.

Yucatangee talked and talked. It talked so much it
heard only itself. Not the river, not the wind, not even
the Wolf. The Raven came and said "The Wolf is
hungry. If you stop talking, you'll hear him. The wind
too. And when you hear the wind, you'll fly." So he
stopped talking. And became its nature, the Eagle. The
Eagle soared, and its flight said all it needed to say.[12]

OK, anyone who has ever met me knows that I never stop
talking for long. Like my father, I enjoy a friendly discussion.
But it's true that the quiet, soaring grace of the eagles pointed
me in a direction those first years after the crash, a direction
of silence, a direction of pulling away from the need to say
the right thing for other people, to hit the right note for other
people, to say or do or be anything for other people. I had to
spread my wings and soar and let the winds carry me where
they would.

One morning in the spring after the crash, I was out on
Medicine Lake, which was close to Golden Valley, Minnesota,
where I lived at the time. I paddled around a bend and lost
my breath when I caught sight of a huge eagle soaring across
the water flying back to its nest. So, from that time on, I'd
always return to that spot on the lake and check in on that
eagle to see what it was up to. I kept that up right until the
week I left Minnesota to live full time in California.

At it turned out, it didn't matter if I stayed in Minnesota
or moved around the country—the way the eagles were
always there for me. Later, I had a chance to visit Sedona,

Arizona, which is not only beautiful, but one of those places that has such a feeling of spiritual power, it's sometimes called a spiritual vortex. I was inside a small chapel on the hill in Sedona, and as I came out I looked up at the famous red rocks of Sedona. A guy in his seventies put his hand on my shoulder.

"You see it, don't you?" he asked me when I turned around to look at him.

"What?"

"The eagle."

And then I did see it. There in the stone, as if it had been carved, was an eagle. It was unbelievable, the most amazing eagle. I had gone to Sedona looking to explore the mysteries of spirituality, but that eagle was as spiritual a presence as any I could come upon. The eagle offers a reminder, as Blake put it, to "Lift up your head!" Be proud and strong like the eagle, and take the long view. I had lived through years in which it seemed that walking forward, taking even one step along the path of the rest of my life, was beyond me. Now I at least began to hope that, even if I couldn't yet take a step, I might spread my wings and be lifted again by fresh currents.

CHAPTER 5

THE AMIGO ROAD HOUSE FINDS ME

he choice to move to California amounted to my admitting to myself that something wasn't working. I haven't gone into it in much detail so far, since it was more than enough to tell about my family and losing them, but I'd already been going through a tough time even before I lost my parents and sister. I'd gotten married young, had become a young father with two children, and my wife and I were right for each other in so many ways. We met in college and went into the Peace Corps in Africa together and worked on an agro-forestry program in the Solomon Islands, where we set up a small egg-laying project. We started with four chickens and built it up from there. The last I heard, the project is still going. Soon we were working a farm together in southern Minnesota. But by the time the plane went down, we had been living apart for over two years and were headed for divorce.

I'll always remember how much it meant to me to have my parents behind me in this rough stretch, when I felt like I'd messed up my life and was wondering if I'd ever get another shot at building a life together with a woman and making it work. Congress was in session in March when my birthday rolled around and my mother went shopping for a birthday card. I pulled it out of the mailbox and was happy they had remembered, but what really grabbed my attention was the image on the card. I took a closer look. It was a picture from somewhere in the Hawaiian Islands that was so stunning and evocative, you wanted to slip into your swim trunks and hit the surf. I knew it was Hawaii because right there in the front was an outrigger canoe parked in a shallow puddle, surrounded by greenery, and in the near distance the emerald blue of an ancient fishpond, built by the original Hawaiians, a row of palms behind it marking the border with the ocean. It was a Hallmark card, but even the printed message meant a lot to me: "Wishing you time to relax, to unwind, to enjoy a quiet hour, and to dream some special dreams. Wishing you everything that will make you feel peaceful and happy and loved."

Hallmark cards were better back then, weren't they?

Below the printed "Happy Birthday," my mother had added "We love you" and signed it "Mom" with a + mark so my dad would know where to write "Dad." He used a light felt-tip pen to write that in, then over on the right, added "David, You have all our love and support. Dad."

The divorce had dragged on and my parents wanted to reach out and give me a little extra support. Later, when I lost my parents and sister in that crash, no one could offer me the same kind of support. The combination of the divorce and its aftermath and the deaths in my family added up to a double whammy. I felt knocked sideways. I knew just what had hit me, but knowing didn't help.

I thought at first I could tough my way through the pain and confusion, the way I would as a wrestler, starved down to weight, struggling against some guy, just the two of us on the mat, with no one there to help. I was trying to prove to myself that I could carry on, that I could stand up on my two feet without my best advisors and support network, and I could fight in the big arena where my father had worked for so long to make a difference. But I always had the feeling that something was off. It wasn't as if I was expecting to wake up one day feeling thrilled by life at all times, the shadows of loss and pain forever banished from view. I just had the hope that the oppressive feeling bearing down on me at all times might start to feel a little lighter. Instead, around the time I decided to move to California, it felt as if it was as heavy as ever.

PULLED UP THE HILL

I started taking trips to northern California, and I was really struck by the beauty of the central coast area, starting with Santa Cruz, two hours south of San Francisco on the northern end of Monterey Bay. The annual golf tournament at Pebble Beach, down the Monterey Peninsula, is less than an hour away and it doesn't get more beautiful than the backdrop there, the placid waters of Stillwater Cove and the Monterey Pines. I would drive around the Santa Cruz area looking at houses and trying to imagine living in each of them. Would I like to live in a house right next to the raging, roaring Pacific Ocean in all its drama? The idea appealed to me a lot. Then again, a bank of fog settles in over that entire coastline much of the time and the damp cold can catch you by surprise.

I took to making regular drives up and down a winding street called Rodeo Gulch Road, popular with bicyclists winding back into the Santa Cruz Mountains. It sweeps along past redwoods, each twist in the road opening up on a stunning new view. I turned onto a street called Amigo Road one day and saw an older man pounding a "For Sale" sign into the ground there at the bottom of the hill. I zipped past him and up Amigo Road, all the way to the top, loving the view of the Pacific below and the sense of being swallowed up by the forest opening up all around. On the way back down, I was almost back to the main road when I noticed that the man pounding in the "For Sale" sign was gone, but he had left behind a box on the sign with flyers.

I picked one up and was blown away by the pictures of the house and its ideal setting. I felt an immediate connection: the redwoods and oaks, the stone columns at the entrance to the place, the sunset view out toward the ocean, the sky over the Pacific coming alive in a riot of pink and purple and salmon and red. The house itself looked charming and rustic. I liked the turret, which gave the place a sort of California mission style that I loved right away, but I also knew it would take a lot of work to remodel and polish it up. I could tell that much just from the brochure. But I had to see for myself.

Driving all the way back up, now looking for the house at the end of the way when it dead-ends, I felt inexplicably drawn up Amigo Road. I felt almost a physical sensation of being pulled along by a magnetic force, even as I had the scary but exciting sense that I had no idea why I was having this feeling. I could not escape a deep certainty in my bones that I belonged at this house I had seen in the picture. I felt that powerful sense of doing just what you need to do at a certain time to make that veer or transition from the same old thing to something fresh and new and exciting and life-giving. I felt a sense of serenity and peace and good energy beckoning, but it was also confusing and amorphous, nothing I could quite identify or pin down. I won't claim I had any clear premonition that this house would become my solace and haven for many years to come—let alone that I would find myself, ten years after the crash, working my tail off to have the place ready to serve as a Wellstone Center in the Redwoods.

Up on top of Amigo Road I was struck by the stillness of the place and the crazy, exciting swirl of smells, the almost overpowering scent of jasmine and orange blossoms wafting over from the orchard, red salvia flowers erupting all over the place. The owner saw me pull into his driveway and park, and he urged me to take a look around the five-acre lot, so I headed out toward the front where a wobbly look-ing little house sat at the front of the property, perched on a rise in just the right place to give it a sweeping view of the gorge cutting its way toward the sea, with stands of pine and oak and redwood rising up the far slope. I sat out front of that little house and stared out at the sea. I felt like a spell had been cast on me. Miles of tree line were all I could see between me and the milky blue Pacific below, and around me was a crazy rush of life, bushes and trees and wildflowers rustling back and forth in a light breeze, seagulls calling in the distance, jays protesting behind me at their ornery best, little twittering songbirds carrying on all around at double-time speed.

First, I heard the screeches. Five or six red-tailed hawks were soaring over the canyon, calling to each other. If you've never seen a hawk that size in flight, talons descended, let me tell you, it's one of those sights that freezes you, it's so startling and dramatic. These big birds moved with such grace and power, I was awestruck. Back in Minnesota I had the bald eagles, and here in California I was going to be kept company by hawks.

Then the first of the hummingbirds made a rush at me. I was on a seat out in front of the little house, and the tiny little bird came whirring up at me like it had been shot out of a cannon. It hit the brakes and pulled into a hover about three inches in front of my nose. It held there, flailing the air, and did its best to stare me down. I stared right back, not wanting to make a wrong move. It felt other-worldly. I really had the sense that I had been magically transported to some other place that was not good old planet Earth. The vibe that immediately seeped in was far too intense for any normal explanation to apply. I saw the buzzing visitation from the hummingbird sentry as a sign—an amazing sign—that I was meant to be in that house.

"Let me give you a tour," the man said, after I'd taken a quick look at the main house. "The house is nice, but the land is special."

He showed me the organic fruit orchard and the giant eucalyptus just behind the house, and then we walked through a gate at the back of the house and were on a small, private trail walking into the forest. Soon we were surrounded by redwoods.

"These are all on the land," he said, grinning and waving his hand in the air to show me. "Your own private redwoods."

I put my hand up against one of those redwoods and felt a calming energy pulsing into my body. It was love at first sight. I knew at that moment I was guided to that place for a reason. There was no turning back. If I missed a sign like the one calling to me to that house, I was really stupid.

The man told me the story of why he'd moved to the Amigo Road house. He said his father had been killed in an accident on the side of the road and he needed a place of special beauty and healing power, a calm and inspiring place where he could find comfort in solitude. I nodded without explaining my own story.

Later that first day at the house, I took a long hike down the private trail leading back from the main house and connecting with a whole network of virtually unused trails running for miles and miles. My mouth was hanging open. All this right out your back door? I remember passing manzanitas with their beautiful red color and crossing a creek at the bottom of the gorge, then exploring the far side and finding wonderful groves of redwoods sloping down toward the creek. What I remember even more about that hike was that I never saw another soul. What magic! Hiking the Santa Cruz redwoods so near the coast and seeing nothing but nature. Later that year walking that same loop, I spotted a bobcat, encountered a group of coyotes, and found a fresh kill that had to be from a mountain lion.

"Where you staying?" the owner of the house asked that first day in a friendly, offhand way.

He was asking if I needed a place to sleep for the night. I didn't, but in a way, his was the better question: This was where I was staying. Amigo Road was my future. We struck a deal in no time and I agreed to buy the place. Less than a month later I came back to take one more look and set everything in order. Then all I had to do was fly back to Minnesota and tell my children, Cari and Keith, that we were moving to California.

LIFE IN THE CALIFORNIA REDWOODS

One thing I found interesting about those first months of living at the Amigo Road house was that I never slept in. There on the edge of a redwood glade, the calm and quiet of the place folded in around you and you slept so well, so deeply and peacefully, the ticklish first light of the day poking in past the trees would pull you awake and you would lie there a minute listening to the first chirping birds of the morning and the call of the quail. Then you would want to bolt out of bed, brew some coffee, and cruise around the grounds of the place, looking for fresh amazements, always coming across something new. Then you would get to making your plans for the morning, deciding which projects you were going to take on, which work needed to get done to make the place even more amazing than it already was.

Some mornings I would start my day by taking the dogs for a walk. They would be barking and hopping around even before I headed for the gate, because your dogs always know what you're thinking, sometimes before you do. I would take them down the trail out the back and down the slope and right into a temperate rainforest—the official name for the type of forest along the northern California coast.

The dogs loved that, and so did I. The trails were a big part of what had brought me there. I walked those trails before I got a full tour of the house. The Amigo grove of trees giving way to this endless landscape, to walk for miles among the redwoods and the scrub oaks and the manzanitas, encountering new wonders every time—one day a trio of huge banana slugs, another day California's version of a gecko sunning itself trailside, another a bobcat passing on the trail, the next a red-tailed hawk swooping past me, talons outstretched, to snag a small rabbit trying in vain to hop away. Then, at the end of the hike, I would be back at Amigo Road. I never get tired of the amazement of coming out of those Soquel redwoods, cool and serene, and back out into the full glory of the sun, looking out at the flat expanse of Monterey Bay beyond the tree line shimmering off in the distance. It gets me every time I hike that route.

I got to work planting. I started with some fruit trees and vegetables, more because I wanted the stuff to eat than any love of gardening I'd identified up to that point. I was stunned to realize how much I loved it out there. The smell of the freshly turned earth, the sight of fresh little sprouts of carrot or basil poking up through the soil line, the planting, the digging, the ritual of turning over the earth and putting things in and watching them grow—I found I loved everything to do with gardening.

There had been two river-rock pillars marking the front gate to the house, and a matching retaining wall lining the road. I loved the look of the polished boulders, some slate gray, others whitish, still others amber, forming a mosaic of color and texture. I wanted to lay new stones and see if I could make pillars and walls that looked even better than those near the front gate. At first I would drive down to a local supply store and handpick the stones one by one and build new pillars and walls. Before long, I would be bringing in truckloads and sorting through them to find just the right place for each stone. Then, we'd use the flat stones for the walkways, with golf ball–size river rocks in between, marking the borders, occasionally inlaying a mandala, or Hindu circle design.

The first priority was the flat-stone pathway through the orchard. At that time there were a few trees there, a plum, nectarine, orange, and an apple tree. Working with my partner, Carlos, I got that first path finished in two weeks and started working on some steps up toward the pool and hot tub using the same style of flat stones inlaid with small river rock to bring out the different textures. The work was hard, grueling even, especially when the sun was beating down, but with every rock we put into the ground, making the place a little more beautiful, I felt a deep sense of satisfaction. I also felt a sense of being pulled forward toward some larger goal or purpose that I didn't even stop to ponder, since I was enjoying focusing on each stone, one at a time, each day of work, one day at a time.

On the north end of the house, looking down on the redwood groves on one side, was a rickety storage shack and below that a broad hillside covered with nothing but weeds and lots and lots of poison oak. I decided to take on that hillside. We dug out a big area for a retaining wall and laid concrete blocks, which we finished with the river rocks. Below the retaining wall, we built steps that went down to a plateau where we laid more flat stones for a floor and put in a stone bench next to a fire circle. Above that we built an outdoor pizza oven, finished in the same river-rock pattern, almost giving it the look of a small chapel. And as the crowning touch on that side of the house, I decided I needed a covered place to sit and eat in the shadows of the redwoods. I could have found a friend to draw up some architectural sketches or hired someone, but that's not my style. Instead, I took the hexagonal trampoline I had bought for the kids and dragged that down there, then simply built the wall around it. Voila! A neat and precise geometric design. Then we built up the walls and put the roof on, and now people who come visit tell me it's the perfect place for theater in the round or weeklong summits.

The beauty of nature can be so healing. Each day when I stirred awake at first light, it was as if the land around the house became my canvas. I had a vision each morning, and I would work all day to bring that vision to life, to finish a piece of the masterpiece. I finished the orchard, adding lime and lemon trees, tangerine and kumquat, two cherry trees, a white grapefruit, another apple, orange, and nectarine, maintaining the commitment to organic farming. The orchard was finished, and then came the organic gardens where I grew vegetables. I was always looking for fresh challenges, even after I had transformed the place into a magic little world where any visitor would be immediately struck by the special energy in the air, brought on by the physical beauty all around, yes, to be sure, but something more than that— something spiritual and healing that gave this special location the ability to bring about changes in how I lived and even who I was.

I had moved far away from Minnesota, but I brought my family with me. Cari and Keith loved their rooms upstairs in the house with a great view. Before I ever made the move, I had talked to my brother, Mark, and knew he was ready to join us in the Santa Cruz Mountains. He bought a house up the slope so we could walk back and forth between each other's houses, dropping in on each other or just knowing that the other was close at hand.

Family tragedy brings you together, but it's not always easy. Mark and I had both lost so much and both felt so much pressure to live up to the example our parents had set for us. Sometimes we crossed wires, but that's just part of being brothers. Mark knows how much I love him, how important he will always be to me. We made a lifelong commitment that whether we were living next door to each other or half a continent away, we would always be there for each other, because we were all that was left of our immediate family, the last two, and we had to stick together.

Some days, Mark would stop by the house and we would head out onto the trails together for long walks through the redwoods and oaks and manzanitas, usually not saying much. But even if we didn't talk, we knew what the other was thinking and feeling, and it was a time of togetherness that I always cherished. That's the great thing about family. Words often didn't even matter. It was being together and sharing something that mattered above all.

Moving to California did involve some readjustments. As Minnesota boys, Mark and I grew up with the Minnesota Timberwolves as our NBA team. One day we decided to make the two-and-a-half-hour drive from Amigo Road to catch a game between the Timberwolves and the Sacramento Kings. We donned our Timberwolves jerseys, like any good fans, and showed up at the raucous, noisy arena and took our seats. We might have been fine if the Kings had won the game, but instead the T-wolves pulled it out and the hometown fans were in a foul mood streaming through the exits. Out in the parking lot, Mark and I attracted a lot of attention in our Minnesota jerseys. Soon we were taking some heavy verbal abuse. We realized we had better rein in our hooting and hollering over the victory and concentrate on finding our car and getting the heck out of there before a loud, foul-mouthed knot of young Kings fans converged on us. It was like old times, like being kids back home in Minnesota, getting into it with fans after a Wolves game.

I WAKE UP FAR FROM HOME TO SEE
THE WORLD IN A NEW LIGHT

Life at Amigo Road was a big step forward for me. I had good times with my brother and my son and my daughter. I had many walks with my dogs on trails that burst forth with a light show of possibilities. I took some workshops on looking within and found some answers that way, too. But through it all, some of my basic wiring was still giving me a lot of trouble. My default position was to want to be alone. In part, that's just who I am. I love people and I can talk you off your stool most days. But sometimes it's almost like something has clicked and flipped over inside me and I just want to sit alone in my bathtub or pull up a chair outside and watch the fog break down into little shrouded clumps, groping their way up the hill from tree to tree, looking as alive as the trees or the hawks above.

Sometimes I'd hear a lot of those clicks telling me I was spent. I'd need to be by myself a lot. The Amigo Road house was great for that, but in some ways, too great. It was easy for me to hide away up there and pull back from the world. That was no way to form new attachments or begin new projects. But for years, it was all I had in me to do. I needed to feel some real currents of excitement if I was going to take on anything really new.

I kept thinking about that birthday card my parents had sent me when I was going through the divorce. I had never been to Hawaii, but the image on that card made me want to go. I wanted to see lines of palm trees. I wanted to see a beached outrigger canoe. I wanted to feel as if I had entered the world that card evoked in me, a world of feeling peaceful and happy and loved, just as the card had said. So I went online, found a good fare, and flew over to the Big Island of Hawaii. I had arranged beforehand to buy an old 1994 Volkswagen pop-top camper for a couple grand. Not a bad price. I figured I could sleep in there and brought along one bag with a bathing suit, a couple changes of clothes, and not much else, but I did remember to bring along that Hallmark card with the Hawaii scene.

Flying into Kona Airport felt like landing on another planet. The plane comes in off the Pacific and drops right down on a vast black lava field that's often baking hot in the sun. I came blinking out of that plane and met the woman who was selling me the VW camper. She smiled at me and gave me a big hug. I felt enveloped, but it was kind of nice to have someone welcoming me. She looked into my eyes in a way that made me feel jumpy, and I tried to laugh it off with a joke, but she kept staring into my eyes, as if looking for something she couldn't quite find.

"You found the Big Island for a reason," she told me. "You have to figure it out. Don't give up until you know what it is."

I was happy to be driving away in the VW. It was an intense encounter, and I had no idea what to make of it. Let's just say I'm not the type to binge on Paulo Coelho books. I believe in signs in our lives, very much so, but I'm a little uneasy sometimes having somebody else tell me which signs I should be focused on.

The camper was belching and backfiring as I drove north up the Queen Kaahumanu Highway. By this time it was dark, but I could still see the outlines of the lava fields around me and feel the force of the Pacific pounding away against lava shores down below on the left. I got to the other side of Kekaha Kai State Park, drove five or ten miles up the highway, and felt the camper start to lurch on me. I hadn't even checked the gas gauge! I assumed the woman had at least left me some gas. No such luck.

You can bet I gave the tire of that camper a good kick when I had to pull over and leave it there. What else could I do? I'm an early riser and like to conk out early, and I was still on California time. I had almost nodded off at the wheel. The last thing I wanted was some hours-long scavenger hunt to find a gas can and get the camper going. I needed to crash right away. So I took my bag with the change of clothes and that old Hallmark card from my parents and threw down a credit card to book a room in the first hotel I found walking away from the camper. The place was fancy, not my first choice, but I was in no mood to care. I was only in a mood to find a bed fast and go facedown, which was just what I did.

I woke up early and had to blink hard a few times to get my bearings. Where the heck had I ended up? I walked outside and that syrupy island air closed in around me like silk. I set off on a little walk to explore the grounds of the hotel and then just kept walking. Hawaii was every bit as beautiful as I'd hoped. The palms rustled in a light morning breeze, but the air temperature was perfect. I kept walking and came around a cluster of trees and almost fell over.

It was too much to believe. I'd wanted to see a row of palms lined up. I'd wanted to see an ancient fishpond created by the old Hawaiians. Now, here it all was. I was staring at the exact vista featured on the card my parents had sent me. Every detail was the same. My mom and dad had never been here—except in spirit through that card—but here on my first visit to Hawaii I felt as if I had found them. They were with me, or at least some important part of them was, some gift of love and support and faith delivered through a tattered birthday card. That gift now filled me. I sank to my knees and could not help crying . . . good tears, happy tears. I felt like I was getting a hug from my parents right then and there.

Paul Wellstone, surrounded by his family, talks to supporters after winning the 1990 primary. *Photo by Brian Peterson/Star Tribune; September 11, 1990*

Daughter Marcia, wife Sheila, and Paul Wellstone make their getaway in 45° below zero windchill. *Photo by Mike Zerby/Star Tribune; December 21, 1990*

Sheared trees stand out in the background as investigators sift through the wreckage in Eveleth, Minnesota, Sunday, October 27, 2002, of the twin-engine plane that crashed killing Senator Paul Wellstone, D-Minn., his wife, daughter, and five others. *AP Photo/Jim Mone, Pool*

A newspaper, candle, and flowers sit among the many remembrances outside Senator Paul Wellstone's campaign headquarters in St. Paul, Minnesota, Monday, October 28, 2002. *AP Photo/ M. Spencer Green*

Memorial service for Senator Paul Wellstone: Cari Wellstone, David Wellstone's daughter, cries during the speeches. On her right is David Wellstone, on her left is Mark Wellstone. *Photo by Jerry Holt/Star Tribune; October 30, 2002*

Eric Reichwald, of Minneapolis, says the Kaddish (Jewish prayer for the dead) beside Paul Wellstone's campaign bus in the parking lot behind the campaign office. Reichwald was a volunteer for Wellstone's 1990 campaign. *Photo by Tom Sweeney/Star Tribune; November 10, 2002*

Dave Wellstone, left, with former First Lady Rosalynn Carter and Rep. Patrick Kennedy, D-RI, talk in Washington, Tuesday, July 10, 2007. Carter and Wellstone were pushing legislation that would require equal health insurance coverage for mental and physical illnesses, when policies include both. *AP Photo/Dennis Cook*

Rep. Patrick Kennedy, D-RI, center, gestures during a rally on Capitol Hill in Washington, Wednesday, March 5, 2008, to discuss the bipartisan mental health parity legislation. Front row, from left, are, David Wellstone, House Majority Leader Steny Hoyer of Maryland, Rep. Jim Ramstad of Minnesota, Kennedy, former First Lady Rosalynn Carter, and House Speaker Nancy Pelosi of California. *AP Photo/Manuel Balce Cenata*

Friends and supporters of the late Senator Paul Wellstone stroll through a five-acre historic site and memorial sculpture garden near Eveleth, Minnesota, Sunday afternoon, September 25, 2005. *AP Photo/Mesabi Daily News, Mark Sauer*

CHAPTER 6

ANOTHER WELLSTONE GOES TO WASHINGTON:

Lobbying for My Father's Signature Issue

---

*M*uch of the last ten years of my father's life were devoted to passing mental health parity legislation. He worked in tandem with Republican senator Pete Domenici to form what he liked to call a political "odd couple." As Deborah Sontag wrote in a *New York Times* article a month before my father's death, "For 10 long years, Domenici and Wellstone have focused their energies on a law that would force health insurers to treat mental and physical illnesses with full parity. They consider it civil rights legislation, but insurers and employers—potent lobby groups who view it as a costly and unnecessary new mandate—have largely succeeded in blocking it."[13]

For my father, it was an issue that hit close to home, as it was for Domenici and many of the other key senators involved. My father's older brother had struggled with mental illness. Domenici's daughter was diagnosed with atypical schizophrenia. Senator Alan Simpson had a niece who committed suicide. Senator Harry Reid's father had also ended his own life.

"There has been a personal, crystallizing experience in each of our lives," my father told Sontag for that article. "You almost wish it didn't have to work that way, that all of us would care deeply anyway about people who were vulnerable and not getting the care they need. But this kind of thing happens a lot in politics for fully human reasons. . . . My energy on this issue is fired by tremendous indignation."[14]

I saw signs of that tremendous indignation all the time. My father would get very frustrated. He used to tell me that people with mental health issues and addiction are a "besieged minority" that few in politics really wanted to go to bat to protect. That October 2002 *Times* article reported that, at long last, the tide seemed to be turning and after years of futile struggle, my father and Senator Domenici were finally close to getting legislation passed, a goal that then seemed "tantalizingly close."

A year later we were still not there. I had thought that, after the crash, the time might be right to get the Wellstone bill passed. Promises were made. Maybe it was naïve of me, but I thought it would really happen. Congress had seemed so close shortly before my father's death and it seemed to me, and to many others, that getting the bill passed in the year after his death would also be an appropriate way to honor him and add to his legacy.

It turned out to be far more difficult than any of us could have imagined, and it left me little choice but to make this fight a personal battle. As I told the Washington-based *Roll Call* for an article thirteen months after my father's death, it had become evident to me after the crash that there was an obligation to continue this work. "David Wellstone has his father's eyes, his father's voice and his father's passion," the article reported. "Now, a little more than a year after Sen. Paul Wellstone (D-Minn.) died in a plane crash, David Wellstone has picked up his father's most important fight."[15]

The article emphasized how impatient I was to get the bill passed that year, even though everyone, including Domenici, claimed that was a hopeless goal. "I don't believe in baby steps," I said at the time. But that article also touched on how the experience of going to work on the parity fight was rewarding for me in some unexpected ways, noting how I had already had "more than a dozen face-to-face meetings with Senators . . . gotten a chance to meet with and talk to the men and women who worked side by side with [my] father, learning things [I] never knew."

That was true. As an example, I remember I was uneasy going into a meeting with Senator John Warner, the Virginia Republican who had been married to Elizabeth Taylor. I never knew how it was going to go when I headed into Republican offices. I didn't know what to expect meeting Warner. I knew he was the chairman of the Senate Armed Services Committee and a former Navy Secretary. I had no idea where he stood regarding my father. I expected a very cordial politeness.

I arrived in his Senate office for our meeting and was ready for a quick handshake. Warner stepped up and hugged me. Instead of that noncommittal mask you get from some senators, even if they're smiling, Warner was beaming and welcoming me like family. He was open and warm. It was a very deep, heartfelt, emotional meeting where I felt the love this guy had for my father.

"I respected your dad and he was a great friend," Warner told me.

After a while, the senator pulled me over to see a picture of him standing there with my dad and told me all about a Senate fact-finding trip they had taken together and the great memories he had from that trip. By the end of the story, Senator Warner had tears in his eyes. So did I. It was a very emotional meeting, one that I didn't expect to have in that office. I expected that in the offices of Democrats who were my father's best friends, like Harry Reid, Dick Durbin, and Tom Harkin, but not on the Republican side.

There was so much goodwill toward my father, such a broad base of consensus in the Senate to live up to promises that had been made just after the plane crash about passing the Wellstone bill as a tribute to my father's work on this issue. I was just certain the deep emotion I was seeing in men like Warner would ensure that this much-needed legislation would finally get on the books. Nevertheless, we came up short. It was a sour defeat. I went home and brooded about it. But there was nothing else to be done. Not then.

The bill never even came up for a vote that year. We'd rallied thousands of supporters all over the country to lobby

for the bill, even getting my dad's green bus out on the road
to D.C. again, but as so often happens in Washington, in-
action killed the bill. However, I was glad that my brother,
Mark, and I had joined together with one of my father's
close associates to found a nonprofit organization—called
Wellstone Action!—to train a new generation of grassroots
activists to learn from my father's example.

THE PARITY FIGHT PULLS ME BACK IN

The earlier defeats on parity really stung. I had to pull away
and try to ignore it all. I was just too frustrated to pay attention to every twist and turn of the various efforts in the
Senate and House to get a parity bill moving again over those
next few years. People would call up now and then and ask
me to do something to help. Sometimes I would. But I really
was not in the fight. I was on the outside looking in. I was
too ticked off to let myself care again. I was in a slow seethe,
which I did my best to ignore.

Then Ellen Gerrity gave me a call in 2007 to ask if I would
get active again. She had worked closely with my father as
his legislative assistant for mental health issues.

"We need you, David," she told me. "There is a bill in the
Senate that they want to name after your dad. It's mental
health parity in name only. He would not support it at all.
We have to do something. Can you get involved?"

"Absolutely," I said.

My blood was boiling. I was ready for action. If they were
going to pass that bill, it would not have my dad's name on

it. They were looking for a way to at least partly fulfill the promise they'd made to get the bill passed the year after my father's death, but they also wanted to keep the health insurance industry happy. Health insurers helped write the bill. They avoided the protections and inclusions my father had insisted on having in the bill. It was so watered down, it was a travesty.

Ellen's call was no fluke. The Parity NOW Coalition that came together to push to get parity passed had been brainstorming. They sensed opportunity. It looked like Barack Obama was going to be elected president in 2008 and both houses were going to have Democratic majorities as well. The point was not partisan scorekeeping. The point was that when the Republicans controlled Congress, it was impossible even to get a hearing on parity. The time was right to make a push. They wanted someone from outside Washington with some national name recognition on the issue to help galvanize the fight. Given my father's visibility on the issue, the Wellstone name carried instant resonance.

I flew out to Washington right away for a round of meetings to get the lay of the land on how the parity fight was shaping up. I attended a bunch of meetings on the Senate side to express my dismay. I made it clear the family did not want this bill going forward under the Wellstone name. They could have still gone ahead with it, if they'd really wanted to insist, but it soon became clear that they wouldn't without the family blessing.

I worked closely on the issue with Carol McDaid, who led the Parity NOW Coalition. We made a good team, Carol and

I. "Oftentimes we could get meetings because Dave was with us that we could not have gotten without him, particularly with senators who were personal friends of his father's, like Harry Reid, like Tom Harkin, like Dick Durbin, all who were in incredibly important positions of leadership," Carol remembers.[16]

It's interesting to discuss those years with her now. When I called her up to talk about this book, she told me she still feels a little guilty about riding me so hard during the parity fight, given what it took out of me. "A little piece of Dave's soul was left behind in every meeting," she said. "He would be either extremely elated or extremely deflated."

My biggest problem was getting my butt there. I had never liked flying, never in my whole life. Then my parents and sister died in a plane crash. The last thing I wanted to do after that was get on a plane, any plane. I avoided flying whenever possible. I would even drive back and forth between Minnesota and California just to avoid flying. That wasn't going to be possible on these trips to Washington. I'd have to take a sleeping pill and get myself through flight after flight after flight. The sleeping pills only helped a little. It still destroyed me to fly. There was just too much there for me. It was all too raw, missing them and being mad at them for being gone, and mad at the world for taking them. It churned me all up inside. It was exhausting. I would come off the plane looking like I'd gone a few rounds with Mike Tyson.

"It always killed me to see him after those flights, because it killed him to fly," Carol remembers. "But having Dave on our side gave us a huge lift. The kind of shoe-leather advocacy we were engaged in is not at all glamorous. You had your natural highs and lows. But we knew we had Dave coming every two weeks, so we would plan around those visits. It forced us to be organized and get the meetings we needed to get. We knew that senators and congressmen were incredibly willing to open up a spot in their schedule to see Dave, often-times over and over. We wanted to make good use of the time he was giving us and we did. He was not being paid for this work. We wanted to make sure his time was well spent."[17]

For a year and a half, I flew back and forth every other week. I had a routine. I'd be at Amigo Road, weeding my garden or taking in the view down by the library house, and then it was like taking a jump in a spaceship, the contrasts were so jarring. I'd drive up to San Francisco, an hour and a half away, and catch a Monday afternoon flight to Dulles Airport in Washington. By the time my cab dropped me off at the hotel in D.C., it would be late and I'd be a wreck. It was a very lonely feeling. I would check into the hotel and, because of the three-hour time difference, it was often hard to get to sleep. Then I'd go, go, go the whole next day until the meetings were all over and I could take some time to myself.

I'd walk to Union Station to get a corned beef sandwich or a slice of pizza or something down in the basement there. It really struck me, the feeling I had of all day long being this sort of mover and shaker, getting accolades, and then strip-ping that off to put on my tennis shoes and jeans and go for a walk. I was more lonely than all those people milling around me at Union Station, even the service workers. At least they had their coworkers to talk to. I was sitting there all alone. It was a feeling of great emptiness. You're up, and then you're down. It was very strange. I felt like a chameleon sometimes, going from Amigo Road to Washington and back, peeling off the suit and walking around the garden in my shorts and flip-flops. It was a strange dichotomy of meetings with senators and then going back to the orchard.

RAMSTAD AND WELLSTONE TEAM UP AGAIN

Our best hope turned out to be working over on the House side. My father had some important allies on the mental health issue among House Republicans, none more important than Minnesota Congressman Jim Ramstad. They were elected on the same day and both took office in Washington for the first time in January 1991. Ramstad was a recovering alcoholic, sober for ten years by the time he was elected to Congress, and he made no secret of that fact. My father had great admiration for the way Jim was forthright in discussing his own experiences with addiction in a way that could help bring attention to the issue and reduce the stigma associated with even talking about it.

Addiction was Ramstad's passion and one of the main issues he focused on in Congress, and that made my father and him important partners. They worked closely together, which brought them together personally as well. Flying back and forth between Washington and Minnesota, they were often on the same flights and their talks developed more and more depth. The friendship they formed meant more than political differences. My father was only two years older than

Ramstad, but I'm told many saw an almost fatherly aspect to his relationship with Jim. Let's just say it clearly went way beyond the collegial. Jim was close to both my parents.

Ramstad had some fun at my father's expense when Dad started thinking about running for president in 2000. He set off in May 1997 on something he called the "Children's Tour," visiting urban neighborhoods of Minneapolis, Baltimore, and Chicago, and rural Appalachia and Mississippi, a tour that evoked memories of the one Bobby Kennedy made in 1966. My father's Senate colleagues liked to kid him about his presidential aspirations, but he insisted that running would bring attention to the progressive issues he championed and went so far as to organize a presidential exploratory committee.

One time in this period, however, Jim and my dad were on the same Northwest flight from D.C. to Minnesota. Jim boarded before my father and went around the plane to talk to other people and organize a hearty rendition of "Hail to the Chief" from all the passengers. My father took his seat, not knowing anything was up, and the passengers launched into song, led by Jim. That was as close as my father ever got to being officially serenaded by "Hail to the Chief." If he'd lived longer, who knows? I can tell you this: He would have definitely run for president the next time.

I discovered for myself in the days after the crash just how close my parents and Jim had become. I called to check my parents' voice mail, not wanting to do it but feeling like it was some kind of duty, just in case anything important needed to be heard. I cleared most of those messages away quickly, but I kept a few that I could just not delete, including one from

Jim, and I'd often hear it again when I called my parents' machine, just to hear my mother's voice on the outgoing message.

On the day of the crash, Jim had heard only fragmentary reports. He'd only heard that my father had been killed, and was broken up about that, but he'd not been aware my mother and sister were also on the flight. He called the house to offer his condolences.

"Sheila, my God, oh my God, I'm sorry," he said. "I didn't know."

There was nothing in that message of official Washington rituals, just one man from Minnesota mourning the death of a fellow Minnesotan he considered a close friend. That message made me feel a strong bond with Ramstad. Given how close my parents had both been to him personally, working with Jim turned out to be a way to get to know my parents better.

It wasn't easy for Jim to support parity the way he did. He took a lot of heat from his Republican party. I respected him for staying true to a real mental health parity bill that would really help people. A lot of Republicans in the Senate were very much against it, but Ramstad always fought the good fight. On almost every visit I made to see him, we spent time figuring out, in particular, how the Republican side of the aisle would vote. In the end, since we had so much Republican support, it was very much a bipartisan issue. We had talks about where to go next in pressing our case. People always tried to strip out little things in the bill, and Jim was never willing to compromise, even in the face of a lot of heat, particularly from his own party.

At first I thought of Ramstad as a friend of my parents, but as time went on I saw him as my friend as well. I had always wondered how it was that some of my dad's better friends in the Senate were Republicans, since they were so diametrically opposed on many political issues, but during this long struggle I learned how much the personal side matters. It's almost like receiving another lesson from my dad. You just never know what will bring people from all different backgrounds together.

MAKING THE FIGHT MY OWN

I was feeling my way, little by little, on some of those first trips to Washington for the parity fight. Early on, going slow was probably the best approach, just making the rounds and contacting people to help them get used to me as the son of the former senator. But I soon got more and more tenacious. We kept running into problems with people who should have known better but supported watered-down versions of the parity bill. This was what really got me into the fight, and I was continually amazed that interest groups claiming to fight for patients' rights were so willing to cut and run, backing a bill designed to please the insurers.

I'd call these people up and scream at them. That might have been impolitic, but it was not something I could hold back.

"Who carried your water all these years?" I shouted at one individual who shall remain nameless. "Where's your backbone? We'll pass the bill without you. You're a disgrace to the organization!"

Then I slammed the phone down. Hey, I was steamed. I realized later it was self-defeating to go at people that hard. Afterward, when I would run into these same people on Capitol Hill or out to eat in the District, they would do their best to avoid me. This was not good. If half of lobbying is being able to run into people out and about in Washington and giving them a little nudge on your priority issue, I had shot myself in the foot. Call it a learning process. I had to be myself. I just needed to tone down some of the rougher edges.

Not that I was going to act like everyone else in Washington. At one crucial point we got a commitment from a key congressman that while he would not support our version of the bill at the subcommittee level, he also wouldn't block it. That counted as good news—sometimes muting the opposition is as important as firing up your people. Then, this very same congressman turned around and led the charge against the bill in subcommittee. He did a 180 on us. Fortunately, it didn't matter in the end. We blew right past him in the Commerce Committee and the bill moved on, but that did not mollify me where his double cross was concerned.

I'm not going to mention any names, but this particular congressman was a six-foot ex-Marine. Just after the vote in Commerce, I was walking with Carol through the tunnel leading from the House side to the Senate side and I saw this congressman walking along. I ran up to him, stood next to him, and plucked at the shoulder of his navy blue suit jacket to get his attention. He turned around.

"Congressman!" I said, not in a quiet voice. "We got ya!"

Then I spun around.

"That probably wasn't a good idea," Carol said as we walked away. "Not good to grab a congressman."

"Duly noted," I said, but we were both still smiling.

One of the dicier aspects of the parity fight was the worry that your coalition might blow up on you. People who were active on parity often had either mental health or addiction issues of their own or people very close to them who did. There was always a healthy concern those issues might flare up. Beyond that, stigma and prejudice slowed down our efforts to campaign for fairness on this issue. People were reticent to speak out. Years earlier, my father would berate some of the key people involved in this struggle for not talking about their own personal experiences of overcoming addiction. Even many years later, a lot of members were still ashamed of their own issues.

The shame was so deeply ingrained that, even when people were out talking about the importance of being public about the issues, they themselves would be very closed about their own experiences. There was never a meeting we went to where someone didn't say "my cousin suffers from schizophrenia" or "my brother suffers from alcoholism," but people still had a deeply ingrained shame about themselves.

I did my best to pick up where my father had left off. People kept telling me I reminded them of him. At first I dismissed it as a mere courtesy, but when I heard it often enough, I was at least willing to concede that it had to be a good thing if I reminded them of my dad . . . even a little bit.

The key on the parity fight was to just keep going. As Carol liked to say, my motor runs a little high, so they made a point of scheduling meetings for me every half hour. That worked just fine for me, always another meeting to pull me on through my day and keeping the down time to a minimum.

When the cafeteria workers at the House of Representatives started to call me by name, that's when I knew I'd been in town a lot. It was like that wherever I went. On the Capitol entrance on the Senate side, some of the women working there would tell everyone how they remembered seeing me come in there when I was "this high." I smiled right back at them. It didn't matter that I was in my twenties by the time my father was elected to the Senate. It was just nice that they remembered.

TEAMING UP WITH A CARTER

One of my favorite partners in the parity fight was Rosalynn Carter, the former First Lady, who chairs the Carter Center's Mental Health Task Force. Her record of advocacy for those suffering from mental illness had long since earned her widespread respect by the time I met her. As she joked when she and I testified side by side to a House subcommittee looking at parity legislation, "I have been working in the mental health field for, I don't like to say it, because it ages me, but for over thirty-five years. That's a long time. When I began, no one understood the brain or how to treat mental health illnesses. Today everything has changed, everything except the stigma, which still holds back progress."[18]

It was great working with Mrs. Carter. It was a real honor to be in her presence. She was so down to earth. She was just extremely disarming, but she had a toughness. When we needed somebody to be tough, we turned to her. She called it like it was.

"To me it is unconscionable in our country, and morally unacceptable, to treat at least 20 percent of our population as though they were not worthy of care," the former First Lady declared, with me at her side. "We preach human rights and civil rights and yet we let people suffer because of an illness they did not ask for and for which there is treatment. Then we pay the price for this folly in homelessness, lives lost, families torn apart, loss of productivity."[19] Sitting next to her and testifying at the hearing on the Paul Wellstone Mental Health and Addiction Equity Act was one of the absolute highlights of the entire experience. I loved watching the way Rosalynn worked. The House members would all come up, wanting to meet her. They spoke warmly to her and recounted memories of working with her and President Carter back during their time in the White House. She was gracious as always, that Southern dignity, but also spoke firmly about the need to move forward with the parity bill. It was awesome. She would smile and then tell them the way it was, nothing diluted, nothing held back.

Have I mentioned yet how nervous I was? The room was packed with all the key advocates and opponents on the issue and though I may have looked fine, in a blue suit and tie, I felt so much nervous energy, it was like someone had punched me in the gut.

"This legislation is very close to my heart and I want to thank Congressman Kennedy and Congressman Ramstad, my good friend who is not here, for honoring my father's legacy in naming this bill," I started off, and if it was pretty obvious to everyone in the room how nervous I was, that was fine with me.

"Nothing represents my father's passion and commitment more than his work to end the discrimination against those who suffer from mental illness," I continued. "Please accept the gratitude of my family and of Wellstone Action for this tribute to my father."

Through it all Rosalynn was calmly seated at my right side in an elegant avocado green jacket.

"I also want to thank Mrs. Carter," I said, and here I turned to my right to face her, "for her many years of leadership on this issue and many others related to mental illness. You and my father often worked together and he was always, always very grateful for your support and leadership."

As I said, I was nervous. Who wouldn't be? I had a good tan going, but my hands looked almost white, the way I kept pressing down the sheet of paper with my prepared remarks. I wanted to make sure I didn't flub any of the lines, and sometimes I read a little fast. But I could feel myself relaxing and my voice growing more commanding as I said, "This law is long overdue, and that is why we are here today," and here I jabbed my finger for emphasis.

"It is time to move forward, for while we wait, people are suffering and dying from lack of care," I said.

"My father fought hard for those who had no voice, and he had a strong personal commitment to help those with mental illness and addiction. Congressional members honored his memory by promising to name the parity bill after my dad, and for that I am grateful. But I do know the kind of man my father was and the kind of parity bill he would have wanted finally passed into law."

I scratched my chin as I geared up for my big finish.

"In the end," I began, then had to pause to take a deep breath. I was that nervous. But I was able to continue: "I am involved, because this is the right thing to do. I want to do my part. This Congress has the opportunity to play a major role in history, and I urge you to do your part to finally enact a strong parity law. Thank you for your courage and your commitment to do the right thing, and know that I'll be there by your side with your efforts to pass this legislation."[20]

I was telling the truth. I was at their side time after time after time as the congressional process worked its way forward.

RAMSTAD AND PATRICK KENNEDY
SPONSOR A BILL

Patrick Kennedy and Ramstad introduced a House bill that was much closer to the mental health parity bill my father had put forward. That kicked my level of involvement up still higher. Some meetings were to gain support for the House bill. Others were to express opposition to the Senate bill. During one of those first trips to Washington during this time, I had my first meeting with Patrick Kennedy,

Ted Kennedy's son, who was first elected to the Congress in 1994.

I was pessimistic going into that first meeting with Patrick. Other than being sons of senators, we didn't seem to have a lot in common. But I had a lot of respect for him. He was basically opposing his own father with the bill he and Ramstad were proposing, which had the kind of full-fledged coverage my father was pushing for all those years. That took courage, going against a major figure in Washington like Senator Kennedy, all the more so when he was your father.

Patrick greeted me warmly and my concerns instantly vanished. Clearly, he had a commitment to this issue. He was very enthusiastic and very high-energy. I came away from that first meeting feeling much more optimistic about our chances of prevailing.

A big step forward came when the House passed mean-ingful parity legislation in March 2008 with Patrick as the main Democratic sponsor and Jim Ramstad as the main Republican sponsor. That was a night to remember. Carol and Ellen and I were up in the gallery together. It was already nighttime and the gallery was close to empty, but down below, the floor of the House was crowded. This was our huge moment. We were so anxious, but also very excited as we looked down at the representatives huddling together and felt a buzz in the air.

Supporters came forward to speak on behalf of the bill, as did opponents. Ted Kennedy was on the floor just below where we were sitting, across the floor from Patrick Kennedy and Jim Ramstad, who were watching the vote. It was looking good, but you never knew. At some point, as we knew we were nearing the end, Senator Kennedy got up and walked slowly across the front of the floor and shook hands with Patrick and Jim. That was his way of congratulating them on the win. The floor proceeded with the vote and the bill passed. Carol and Ellen and I were thrilled. Several House members pointed up at me in the gallery and gave me big thumbs-up signs. Others just waved or smiled. I'm told that's pretty rare, and it really meant a lot to me.

But the victory only counted if we could use it as a battering ram to get the Senate to agree to a comparable version. I would put my head together with Ramstad and Patrick Kennedy often on how best to make that happen. On almost every one of my visits to Washington, we would have meetings with Patrick and Jim to talk strategy and make sure we were all on the same page.

Patrick was very gracious and thankful for my involvement, which did make me feel good. I knew he wasn't just saying it. A little later on, I went to his House office and saw that he had mounted a picture of the two of us on his wall, him and me at one of the parity events we'd organized. That made me feel proud. Here was a guy who was sought after by everybody, who had all kinds of pictures of himself with famous people, and he decided to stick one up there of him with his arm around me. That, for me, was a *Wow.*

Patrick and I got to know each other well. We started to think like each other—and had some of the same wild ideas. Both of us were confident that we could win the debate on the merits—the problem was being heard. We were always worried that the clock would run out on one session of Congress and we would not get a chance to be heard. We'd be shut down once again, left to try to bring it back one more time. So we were brainstorming ways to get more attention focused on the issue.

"We've got to chain ourselves to the Key Bridge!" Patrick declared at one point. "You and me! Civil disobedience!"

He could see I loved the idea.

"We can stop the traffic and hold up signs saying: 'People aren't getting care and are dying.' That will get the media to write about this."

He and I talked about that idea in detail. We seriously did think about it. As I walked back to the hotel that night after mulling over the idea of chaining myself to the Francis Scott Key Bridge, it made me think about my father. I remembered the time when, as a young Carleton College political science professor, he had locked the college trustees inside until they agreed to divest from anyone doing business with South Africa.

The feeling was always strong in this period of having my father at my shoulder when I made the rounds in Washington. My mother, too. Any time I could carve loose some time, I would free myself from duties and go for a walk myself along the National Mall in Washington, up and back, up and back, letting my thoughts wander. My folks had told me years earlier that their favorite thing to do in Washington was to go for a drive. At first they'd cruise around in their old Chrysler LeBaron convertible, and later it was a red 1980s Ford Mustang they had for five or six years. They would put the top down and drive around the Mall at night. Occasionally during those visits to Washington in the years after they were gone, I would retrace their path. It'd be so late when I finished a day of meetings, it would be getting dark. I'd go for a walk on that same route my parents had driven and think of them. I would look up at the Capitol all lit up and the Washington Monument and the Lincoln Memorial and take in how beautiful it was, and think about my parents. I knew it was kind of dangerous, but it was just something I wanted to do.

CHAPTER 7

GETTING THE WELLSTONE BILL
ON MENTAL HEALTH PASSED

he Washington heat would close in on me. It would be late on a long afternoon of meetings that had left me feeling drained and sometimes defeated. We'd be walking across a street and I'd get hit with a blast of hot, humid air and feel like I was melting. It made me want to jump into a shower. It made me want to be at Amigo Road with the dogs or sitting out back under the redwoods. Then afternoon would sink into evening and I'd be walking alone to dinner, on a hot, sweaty D.C. evening, pushed down by a fresh sense of disappointment. It was one of the most up-and-down experiences I've ever been through, the fight for parity. So many times I went to bed feeling great only to wake up to feel the rug had been pulled out.

I remember one series of days in particular when I'd flown in at a pivotal time in the fight. The day before had gone well and it was looking good, and suddenly it was gone. I walked alone in the heat and tried to bake away the disappointment. I got back to the hotel and stood there looking at myself in the mirror.

"What must my father have felt like at a moment like this?" I stood there asking myself in the mirror.

The pressure I felt leveled against us in that fight was intense and well organized, but this was something my father had faced all the time. Like when he helped lead the charge in the Senate to defeat an amendment that would have allowed drilling in the Arctic and worked to have the Coastal Plain in the Arctic Refuge declared a wilderness. Standing in front of that mirror in a Washington hotel room, after another day of fighting for parity, I had a sudden flash of feeling that maybe I understood a little what it was like for my father at the end of a long day to have that feeling of being alone looking into the mirror.

The situation that weekend was especially critical. Meaningful parity legislation had languished, bogged down by the meddling of lobbies and the sensitivity of the issue. We did have the strong bill in the House named for my father, but in the Senate we were up against the momentum created by the insurance plan opponents, a formidable giant, and all the mental health groups who had abdicated on many of the important principles of the strong bill. We had often been advised to give in and compromise. But we never did. We may have been outnumbered and outspent, but no one could fight harder than we were fighting for what was right. We felt we were making progress. We were gaining more supporters.

Then the financial crisis really kicked in. As *Time* magazine reported the week of September 22, 2008, "The dominoes fell one right after another: the demise of Lehman Brothers tipping into the rushed sale of Merrill Lynch to Bank of America, followed by the federal takeover of AIG. Then, the desperate credit crunch of Wednesday caused the emergency maneuvering by the Federal Reserve and the Treasury on Thursday and Friday. In a week, the financial crisis of 2008 changed everything—and now comes the cleanup: if the Administration's $700 billion Wall Street bailout plan is approved by Congress, the United States will see changes to its political economy that were unimaginable a week ago."[21]

A big omnibus bill would be going through, the bailout package, and if we could get a good parity bill passed as part of that, it would be smooth sailing. The president had already said he would sign parity legislation. It all came to a head that fall. I was in Washington, making the rounds, and a win was so close we could taste it. We were all so ecstatic, certain the bailout bill was going to pass and with it parity. I went to bed one night thinking we were there, and woke up to the news that the House had caved.

Jackie Calmes was scathing in summing up the situation in the *New York Times* on September 29:

The collapse of the proposed rescue plan for the teetering financial system was the product of a larger failure—of political leadership in Washington—at a moment when the world was looking to the United States to contain the cascading economic crisis.

From the White House to Congress to the presidential campaign trail, the principal players did not rally the votes they needed in the House. They appeared not to comprehend or address in a convincing way an intense strain of opposition to the deal among voters. They allowed partisan politics to flare at sensitive moments.

If there was any doubt that President Bush had been left politically impotent by his travails over the last few years and his lame-duck status, it was erased on Monday when, despite his personal pleas, more than two-thirds of the Republicans in the House abandoned the plan.[22]

───※───

CRUNCH TIME FOR PARITY

The push to get a bailout bill was both an opportunity and an obstacle for us. We always had to worry about getting thrown under the bus. We always had to fight to put on pressure to make sure the Wellstone bill was not watered down.

An October 1, 2008, *New York Times* editorial explained the legislation:

───※───

Congress is within a whisker of passing a sound and fair-minded bill to require that group health insurance coverage for mental illness and substance abuse be

*provided on the same terms as coverage for physical
illnesses. It would be a shame if the legislation, which
caps more than a decade of struggle to achieve mental
health parity in insurance coverage, were allowed to
die while Congressional energies are focused on the all-
consuming economic crisis.*

*The bill would not require employers or health
plans to cover mental illness or drug or alcohol abuse.
But if they do, the treatment limits and financial
requirements could be no more restrictive than those
that apply to medical or surgical benefits. A 1996
law had required parity in setting annual and lifetime
spending limits, but insurers found ways to circumvent
it. The new bill closes loopholes by requiring parity in
deductibles, co-payments and out-of-pocket expenses—
and in setting treatment limitations, such as the maxi-
mum number of doctor visits and days of coverage
allowed.*[23]

Given that the bailout bill containing parity had been
endorsed by President Bush, mental health advocates, business groups, and the insurance industry, among others, and
versions of parity had been approved by wide margins in the
House and the Senate, the holdup was unconscionable.

"Is there a statesman who can push this worthy parity
legislation through to final passage before adjournment?" the
Times editorial lamented.

With three sponsors of the parity bill (Senator Pete Dominici
and Congressmen Jim Ramstad and Patrick Kennedy) set to

retire, and Senator Ted Kennedy seriously ill, we knew the time was truly now or never to get parity passed. Many of us were lobbying vigorously. The global economy was tanking and we knew a bailout bill needed to pass. To give an idea of how complicated things got, a bailout bill without parity attached failed to pass the House as competing interests lobbied on both sides.

It was the nature of the beast. Promises were made to propel bills through committee. The hard part was working with the senators and the representatives on either side of the aisle who were going to go into conference committee and put these two bills together. A lot of that work was where the angst came because by that point it was out of your hands. You hoped these people would present your arguments and not cave in. Then after that got done it was a matter of how do we actually get it passed. The bailout was our big chance.

The pressure was so intense. Remember, this was the end of the world if the bailout bill didn't pass. That's how it was being presented. President Bush and Vice President Cheney were both working the phones, putting the pressure on key Republicans to step into line. Tony Fratto, a deputy White House press secretary, told the press, "I think everyone with a phone is calling to see if we can shore up a member who may be skeptical of the proposal."[24]

Treasury Secretary Hank Paulson made the rounds, putting out the appropriate doomsday scenarios, and told the press that week, "We need to put something back together that works. . . . Our tool kit is substantial, but insufficient."[25]

The balance was so delicate, we had to do things we weren't even sure we wanted to do. I'm not talking about breaking legs or anything. But sometimes you had to keep your lips sealed in a way that felt uncomfortable. Toward the end of negotiations in the Senate, I was able to get a meeting with a high-level senator, who confided that a deal was in the works to get the bill through the Senate. He said it was imminent. He also said that I needed to keep quiet about this imminence or risk derailing it. I was not even to tell close colleagues in the fight. This was difficult for me. I'm not sure I'd do it again. But at the time it seemed necessary and in the end the strategy did work.

It was a classic Washington finish in a way. On September 29, 2008, the House failed to pass a financial bailout package, one that did not contain parity. That forced Congress to stay in session. Two days later, on October 1, the Senate passed parity as part of its financial bailout package, using the original Patrick Kennedy/Jim Ramstad House bill as the vehicle for the package. Then two days after that, the House passed parity as part of the financial bailout package and President Bush signed the measure into law.

The *New York Times* summed up the significance of our win on the issue in an article by Robert Pear that week under the headline "Bailout Provides More Mental Health Coverage," explaining:

―――∞∞∞―――

More than one-third of all Americans will soon receive better insurance coverage for mental health treatments because of a new law that, for the first time, requires equal coverage of mental and physical illnesses.

The requirement, included in the economic bailout bill that President Bush signed on Friday, is the result of 12 years of passionate advocacy by friends and relatives of people with mental illness and addiction disorders. They described the new law as a milestone in the quest for civil rights, an effort to end insurance discrimination and to reduce the stigma of mental illness.[26]

It's important to emphasize that at the very end, when it could still really have gone either way, Harry Reid and Dick Durbin both fought very hard for this bill. They both wanted the bill desperately. They knew it was the right thing to do. Plus, they also wanted to get it passed for my father. Harry and Dick, I want to thank you for always being there for me when I called you in this period. I know I got pretty amped up at times. It's just my way. But we did some good work together, didn't we?

Tom Harkin is another one I have to single out for thanks. He was so loyal to my father's memory and always made me feel so comfortable every time we talked. He worked the back room, as they say, and did it energetically and effectively, working to make sure we could go forward with a bill that could legitimately be called the Wellstone bill.

People kept thanking me for all the work I did on parity and that was great to hear, but I felt thankful to a lot of other people for what they had done. My contribution only made a difference because of the vast amount of work they had already done and continued to do in tandem with me. Patrick

Kennedy kept the House bill strong so that it set a high bar for what the final bill would be. This gave us enormous leverage in the Senate. Jim Ramstad did the same. In the end, the people who said they would come through, did. I hope when I'm out and about talking about this book I get a chance to thank many of you face-to-face who worked so hard in this period. I can't thank you all here.

Carol McDaid would joke later about how usually they say that in Washington if you want to find someone to trust, get yourself a dog. Maybe it's not as bad as all that, not as cutthroat, as they say, but either way, the bond of friendship and trust I was able to develop with Carol and others in this struggle was very important to me. It might have been the only thing at that point in my life that could have given me any feeling of making progress in recovering from the pain of losing my parents and sister in that crash.

"You were able to regain a sense of purpose and passion that had been missing," Carol observed later. "Or at least a sense of passion you hadn't connected to in a long time. It seemed like you got in touch with that. And it forced me to do the same thing: Human doing instead of a human being."[27]

A CALL FROM SENATOR KENNEDY

By the time the parity legislation was finally passed in October 2008, twelve years after my father had introduced the Senate version of the bill, I had been personally lobbying on Capitol Hill for many years. As I said at the time, "I'm ecstatic. Amazing. I want to pinch myself. In my family, this was a huge moment. To have my dad's legacy be this law is a great thing."[28]

It was a good win. This was one of those rare laws that would really help people. Knowing that gave the victory a feeling that was very pure. It's the way the system is supposed to work. How do you help people? You get some Republicans, you get some Democrats, and you get a bill. It also made me think of my father. What would he ever have done after being a senator, if you could get wins like this, helping enact change that really made a difference in people's lives? I think he would never have given it up. He would have been a senator until he couldn't any more.

Back home in California at Amigo Road, it all took a while to sink in. I enjoyed having more time at home to catch up on work. I was in shorts one day, out picking fruit in my little orchard, when I got a call from an East Coast number I did not recognize.

"Senator Kennedy would like to call you in ten minutes," a voice said. "Would that work?"

I looked around at the stands of fruit trees and said, "Yeah, I could make ten minutes work just fine." It was a little nerve wracking waiting those ten minutes. I was excited and also a little nervous. It had been a battle. Senator Kennedy had been a supporter of the version of the Senate bill I found too watered down, so we'd been on opposite sides on that one. I didn't really know what the call was going to be about.

"David, your dad would be so proud of you," Senator Kennedy told me on the phone that day. "Your spunk and spirit reminded me of your dad."

"Thank you, Senator," was all I could think to say.

I was really overwhelmed.

"I knew you had to put up with a lot and I want to thank you," Senator Kennedy told me.

I am never one to be starstruck, but I freely admit to being awed by that exchange with Senator Kennedy. He was just so generous with his praise. It was humbling. And at that point, talking to him, me in my shorts in my Santa Cruz Mountains orchard, the senator back East, I realized for the first time how big this thing had been. I started to really grasp it. It had all been so surreal in many ways. Senator Kennedy's call helped me to get some perspective on it. Being thanked in that way by him for me was huge.

A month later I was weeding in the garden and came inside to check my messages. One was from Ellen. She was calling to say Senator Kennedy had passed away. I turned on CNN and watched hours of coverage—the fourth-longest-serving senator in U.S. history, last of the Kennedy brothers, one of the most effective legislators ever. One month earlier he'd been on the phone thanking me for my work on parity.

CHAPTER 8

EXPECT SETBACKS AND FAILURE
ON THE ROAD TO RECOVERY:

Place Your Stone Well

---

*T*he parity fight was important because it was about doing the right thing for others, but it helped me, too. It gave me a cause. More than that, it gave me a purpose. As exhausted as I was some days after making the rounds in Washington, I always had the feeling of everything being for a reason. It was hard when the battle was finally over. Yes, we'd won, but now what? For so many months I'd been locked in, going hard on this, always focused on the next meeting, the next strategy session, the next cross-country flight that was going to throw me for a loop. There was a huge letdown when that was all behind me.

I went back to Amigo Road, spent time with Cari and Keith, and went for walks in the redwoods with my dogs. Yet I couldn't escape a feeling of emptiness. For a period of my life, having time alone on the redwood trails with my dogs was what I needed most to move on with my emotional healing. Then a time came when it was relationships that helped to move me forward and get reengaged. The mental health parity fight gave me that. I was engaged and active and I also made very good friends. We had a real feeling of camaraderie. All through that time, I would meet people my dad had known well and respected and they would smile at me and say, "Hey, you're good at this." That made me feel close to my dad and opened things up on a deeper level. I started making some meaningful friendships

Back at Amigo Road, I missed that camaraderie and engagement. I thought of good friends like Carol and Ellen. They worried about the toll the parity fight was taking on me and tried their hardest to get me to agree to come out for a hamburger or take in a baseball game on one of my visits to Washington. And when we talked, it wasn't just rehashing that day's meetings or the strategy we needed to follow. No, by the end of the day we'd had enough of that. We talked about life. We talked about real matters of the heart. We talked to each other from the depths of our souls. Those friendships will always stay with me. Great friendships like that help you to heal.

So often in the years after the crash leading up to this point, I would think I had made some progress, only to feel it slipping away again, like a rug being pulled out from under me. It was almost a physical sensation of wanting to topple right over. The parity fight was the most dramatic example of this—during the heart of the battle I felt as if I had pushed past all of that, only to find that once my days in Washington were over, I was once more back at square one, feeling hollow inside all over again. I was so tired of feeling like I had holes inside myself and couldn't stop wishing they would just go away.

It wasn't to be. Life doesn't work that way. You choose to live on and believe in life again, or you don't. Either way, the holes are still going to be there. They might swallow you up now and then. That's just a reality you have to face. It's best to accept that and then look at the rest of the picture. Oftentimes that means something as simple as not being afraid to look for the good in things and people.

I spent years trying to fill a void. I had to live through countless setbacks to begin to learn what was going to work in helping me move forward and what was just wasting time. I would be seized with a sudden intense desire just to call my mom up on the phone and talk with her for a few minutes, to hear her voice, to tell her about my day or about how my son and daughter were doing. As I've mentioned before, for the longest time I would call my parents' answering machine just to hear her voice. Even when I stopped doing that some months after the crash, I still felt the impulse to make that call.

Instead of letting my grief wash over me, I would try to distract myself by doing more work or taking the dogs for a long walk on the beach or going to a hockey game. I'm not embarrassed that it took me many years to discover that you can't fill the void on the golf course. You can't fill it by aimlessly spending money on something like a new T-shirt. You can't fill it by going out to eat instead of cooking at home and being reminded of meals with the family. You can't even fill that void by absorbing the beauty of a forest or a sunset. You can only start to fill that void when you realize all that matters is what you find inside yourself. I needed to let that grief wash over me if I wanted to be whole and have a full life. I needed to embrace the grief and realize it does wash over and I am all right.

BACK TO THE ANCIENT HAWAIIAN FISHPOND

I found myself craving more of the feeling I'd had in Hawaii when I stumbled on that ancient fishpond I'd first seen in a birthday card my parents had sent me. I'm not a regular churchgoer, but I believe in the spirituality of a special place. I believe the pure and piercing beauty of a place can open up in us a greater sense of awareness or calm or perspective that can help point us in the right direction. I feel that at my Amigo Road home all the time and I'd felt it there on the Big Island of Hawaii, the palms swaying, the surface of the fishpond dappling in the sea breeze. I went back to visit that spot in Hawaii again and to say a prayer there to my mom and dad.

I spent a lot of time alone during my many years of recovery following the death of my parents and sister. I saw my ex-wife and, of course, I often saw my son and my daughter, but still, in an important way I was always a loner. Time alone was as basic a need for me as sleep was for other people, and I needed my eight hours a day—and more. It was hard for me to trust anything.

For all of the beauty of the house on Amigo Road, it didn't feel quite right, me having it all to myself so often. The magic is not meant for one person alone. Such crazy beauty needs to be shared with others, to look out at a sunset together or watch Orion slowly twisting down toward the Pacific over the long hours of a warm summer evening, to walk the dogs in the redwoods together or grill up dinner. Of course I loved it myself, but I still felt a deep sense of uneasiness inside me. I could not shake the fear that getting close to someone again could bring more of the pain I felt in losing my parents and sister. That's what it really was more than anything. I was afraid of that. I realized I just wasn't ready to be there for another person the way I knew I wanted to be. I still needed far too much time by myself.

But after some more time alone at Amigo Road, retreating from the world, it hit me that I wasn't happy pulling away from the world, either. Then it dawned on me that I hadn't been able to feel anything at all. It wasn't so much that I felt sad or afraid, but that I felt nothing. I had gone from the pain to being stuck with no emotions. The fear of ever reliving my grief over the loss of my parents and sister had led me to shut everything down. It was an emergency response: Feeling nothing was better than opening myself up to be hurt again.

But I wanted more than that. I wanted the bad with the good. I wanted all of it. I finally realized that you have to be able and willing to feel pain in order to feel happiness. You have to be open to it all to feel the myriad of emotions. If you want joy in your life, then say hello as well to disappointment. Every relationship is going to have its painful moments, its difficult dynamics. I had been conning myself to think that I could live without really living, that I could be present in a relationship without taking any risks. Opening up and being vulnerable is so hard, but also so, so necessary.

That's true as a parent, too. Being a good father to Cari and Keith didn't just mean showing up for games or getting dinner taken care of. Being flat emotionally wasn't going to cut it. You have to be emotionally alive in order to be there for your kids. If you're flat and empty feeling, you're not going to be much fun to be around. No one is going to want to have any real, in-depth conversations with you, not even your son and daughter, maybe especially not your son and daughter. They know when something's going on. They know in about twelve milliseconds if you're not fully present.

If I didn't make some changes in my life, I was going to lose out on the opportunity I had while my daughter and son were still at home. If we didn't make some emotional headway now while they were both around, then it would be a lot harder—and a lot less likely—later on. That sense of urgency kept prodding me until finally it led me to begin opening up.

Cari and Keith were always my hidden salvation. They don't know it, I don't think. Up until now I've never put the truth into words. But they, more than anyone, were the ones who helped me get through the toughest times. So many days, when I was at my lowest point, all I had to do was think of them and it kept me going. Just the thought of them. Just picturing their faces. The thing I'm the most proud of in life is the relationships I have today with Cari and Keith.

I tried as a father to think of experiences from my own childhood that went awry, and make things different for my kids. I had never forgotten my disappointment as a boy when my dad and I found out the scalpers were charging way more than we could afford for tickets to go see the Purple People Eater–era Minnesota Vikings led by quarterback Fran Tarkenton. I've made a point of getting Keith and me to as many Sharks games as possible. Why not? It's just over the hill, we both love hockey, and one of these years my boy Jumbo Joe Thornton is going to take them to the Stanley Cup finals.

It's funny, the day of the game, you're thinking about getting there right at game time, the way you like to, to beat the traffic by making your entrance after just about everyone else is inside and then sliding right into your seats after the anthems and just before puck drop. You think about a big hit against the boards or a wicked spearing glove save or a slap shot that goes wide, and that's what you talk about, too, you and your son. But later on, looking back, all of that stuff just fades out of the picture. You look back and think of sitting side by side on the drive to the game, just the two of you, time together, talking about the day, or just sitting silently, knowing you're together.

Cari was about to graduate in 2009 and go off to college at San Francisco State, which meant Keith would be off, too, within a few more years. I started to feel a deep sense of some panic building up and occasionally had to vent and blow off steam. Actually, forget the "some panic" stuff. I'd have full-on panic attacks at times. Really. I was that guy. I'd be standing there in the middle of a full-scale panic attack, saying out loud, "My God, I'm losing my kids! My God, I'm losing my kids!"

Mind you, I was saying this during Cari's high school years—a period when she and I would talk on the phone two or three times every day. Her first semester up at SF State, we continued along at that same pace. Yes, she was a daddy's girl, and we were both proud of that. Yet I knew I had to give her some space. It was hard and it was scary. I couldn't shake that deep-down fear that once again I was losing a family member. But I realized that this experience was good for Cari. She needed time and space to grow.

I felt like when it came to Cari and Keith, I had to lead by example, not words. I could always talk. The words were sharp. The words hit the mark. The words always flowed easily. But I started feeling like I had become a version of those very folks my father had chastised earlier for being out there in the fight but not being public about their own issues. How could I be this public leader, rallying the troops for the cause of mental health, when in my own life I was so emotionally shut down? I wanted to show my children by example that you can deal with adversity in life and overcome tragedy, because life is full of that. They saw me doing the work for parity and getting the awards on parity, and I wanted them to see that I was moving forward in my own life, too.

Around this time my brother became a father for the first time, making me an uncle again. A while later, Mark and his wife, Jill, and the baby, Bode, came to stay with me at Amigo Road for a couple weeks. I fell in love with Bode immediately, the energy, the innocence, the laughter. I was just blown away by this little life. He would say, "Uncle Dave, Uncle Dave," all day long and the words became music to my ears. I never could get tired of that. Bode reminded me of what's important in life. The day they left and I stopped hearing "Uncle Dave" echoing down the hall, it gave me a fresh jolt of feeling hollow and empty inside and knowing it was time to fight my way forward emotionally.

Funny how life is. My dad had a former student named Rick Kahn who used to come to the house and babysit me when I was ten years old. When he was older, Rick became my father's best friend and confidant. He was a great friend to him. Then later on Rick became all that and more to me. He's a very close friend, a confidant, really my Rock of Gibraltar at times. I could call him at some of my worst moments and count on him to be there for me, offering me calm and low-key advice or always knowing when the moment was right to tell me what my dad or my parents would have had to say about a particular situation. It really underscores the importance of trust and faith in healing. You need people in whom you can have total and complete trust and also faith, meaning faith that they have no other motive than to help you. It was much like politics. My dad used to tell me that the single most important thing in politics is trust, because that's the hardest thing to find.

PLACE YOUR STONE WELL

The Amigo Road house in the Santa Cruz Mountains taught me that you can be on a mission and have a higher purpose even if no one else knows about it and even if you yourself don't know at first. Everything I did in years of work on the house was step by step, bit by bit, never with a grand plan. When I first moved into the Amigo Road house, it made sense to start working to make it nicer. I took a deep, healing pleasure in laying all those stones with my partner Carlos. I laid a few, then some more and some more. I couldn't stop. It turned into an endless pursuit, first months and then years of getting fresh truckloads of stones dumped on my drive-way and working to lay them all over the grounds.

If someone had told me at the outset that I would find peace through my laying of stones, I'd have laughed that off. But I did find peace. I did find healing. I did find inner meaning. And the stones remain. They combine with the fruit trees and the herb gardens and the outdoor pizza oven and all of the other special details of the place to provide a map of my recovery—and, I hope, to lay the foundation for the recovery or revitalization of many of you who read this book and maybe get a chance to visit Amigo Road.

As I look back on it, each piece of the puzzle, each little project, had its own start and finish and yet the finish always led to the next piece. There were the orchards and the gardens. There was the bocce ball court. There was a massage room with beveled-glass windows. There was a library house with the best view on the land. There was the putting green back near the rear gate leading out onto the redwood trails. There was the stone-covered outdoor pizza oven and gazebo. There was the art therapy area, eight individual high-backed chairs overlooking a redwood grove and offering an ideal spot for tapping creativity. Each of these spaces in and of itself was just a part of the whole, but if you looked back at the mosaic once it was complete, it gave you an eerie feeling of it all coming together absolutely right with the ping of perfection.

"You're an artist," a lot of people would tell me after getting a look around the Amigo Road grounds.

I'd laugh that one off.

"I couldn't draw a stick figure!" I'd say.

"But you're an artist," they would say. "Look at the way all these different elements come together."

I came to see that they had a point. It all flowed so seamlessly together it was as if it was all meant to be, only with no forethought, only intense attention to each of the details one by one by one. Laying each stone, I never saw it as part of an intricate master plan. I could never have dreamed up an intricate master plan. I just saw a place for the stone that seemed right and put it down. Then placed another stone in its rightful spot. And another. And another.

My favorite sculptor, the one-eared Michelangelo—or was that Da Vinci?—had a great line about the creative process: "Every block of stone has a statue inside it and it is the task of the sculptor to discover it," he said.

I looked back at the way the pieces had all discovered themselves at Amigo Road, and only when I had a complete whole in front of me and the parts started fitting together did I say to myself: *Wow, my life has been like that.*

I saw the way that my life, too, was full of all these different, segmented parts. Only at Amigo Road all the pieces fit together just right. In my life, the different pieces felt more like different pieces than one greater whole. The whole picture had not been painted. It had not been finished. That would not be possible while I was shutting down inside in some ways. I wanted to go further in this direction of a renewed depth of connection and feeling for my family. I wanted the mosaic of my life to grow. I started thinking about my kids having kids and what it would be like to be a grandfather and how I wanted to be living my life as a grandfather. I wanted to start down that road. I understood the crucial need for healing to start with me. If not now, with me, then when?

CARRYING ON MY FATHER'S LEGACY,
MY OWN WAY

This book is my tribute to my parents and my sister ten years after the plane crash. I wouldn't want it to come across as a straightforward homage that tries too hard to present an idealized version of my dad and his legacy because that is the last thing my father would want. My parents didn't raise me that way. They always insisted on absolute honesty, even to the point of painful honesty, and an eye toward the possibilities of the future, not too much of a focus on the past.

Along the way in these chapters, I have offered glimpses of what it was like to have the famous fighting progressive Paul Wellstone as a father, playing two-on-two football with him and the neighbor kids or heading out with him for yet another organizing meeting or picket line. I have tried to be as direct and honest as possible in describing the pain and confusion I felt after the tragedy that claimed his life and that of my mother and sister. I have gone over the fight to get the Wellstone bill passed in Congress to ensure mental health parity.

But when I describe this book as a tribute, I have in mind something much more than these glimpses. My father centered his convictions on the idea that if you worked hard for change, if you were resourceful and patient and trusting of other people's better natures, good things would come. The patience part is key. My father, in fairness, was not always the most patient of men in the sense that most people think of as patient. He was true and unfailing in his convictions. That's a kind of patience. But he also hated to wait. He hated deadlock and stalemate. It drove him up the wall.

I'm the same way. I'm an energetic person. I like to keep active. I like to do a lot of work on a lot of different projects, but I get jumpy if I have to wait too long. Call it attention deficit disorder or just a basic restlessness; either way, you get the idea. It's just the way I'm wired. But for many years, during the period I've described in this book, I was in a sense always waiting. I was waiting for time to offer me a path forward. I was looking for a way to honor my parents and sister by never numbing out the pain of missing them every single day, but also to have energy and vision to put into finding and living out a fresh new direction for myself. That, I think, is the ultimate legacy of my father: *Find a way to energize yourself and others for the way ahead.*

I'm not the political animal my father was. I don't know if it's a matter of the style of politics having changed so much in the ten years since my parents and sister were killed in that plane crash, with so much anger and venom and cynicism in the air now, or if the political arena is just not my thing. I'm not at all inclined to follow in my father's footsteps and run for office. My brother and I founded Wellstone Action after the crash to carry on my father's work in bottom-up politics and grassroots organizing and to train generations of new organizers to get to work on behalf of change. That's an important aspect of my father's legacy, and Mark and I are proud we've been able to get so many people engaged and energized for struggles in the years to come via Wellstone Action.

I've also been very pleased to see the way that Al Franken has worked to carry on my dad's legacy in the Senate, in terms of both walking the talk and championing the issues that were most important to my father. Every time I go to D.C., I go in and see Al and it's like going back into the kitchen—it's hugs and first names and smiles, almost like it was when I would talk to my dad, just right past the trivial stuff and on to what mattered. Al has been great on my father's signature issues, especially domestic violence and mental health. He and his wife, Franni, have taken that fight on as a duo in a way that reminds me of the way my parents took on the same issues.

My dad always used his position to fight injustice and make the world a better place. He did that when he was a political science professor at Carleton College and he did that on a larger stage in the Senate. I've found that because of who I am, I get a larger stage as well, and it's really important to stay true to myself, not just talking the talk but walking the walk. I thought that once we were successful getting mental health parity legislation passed and signed, that battle would be over. But even now, with the law passed, mental illness continues to be stigmatized. We've seen foot dragging on getting final regulations established. Final implementation is a battle that still needs to be waged. Rosalynn Carter and Patrick Kennedy and many of the others I worked with before are still waging that fight, and I'm sure I'll continue to chip in to do what I can on that front.

But above all, I hope this book will bring alive my father's legacy in a way that transcends politics and has more to do with how we live our lives. I want to summon my father's energy and commitment as a living, breathing presence in the here and now and use it to inspire me not to follow my father's example, but to go my own way along my own path, energized by the certainty that in finding my own ways to work to make a difference in others' lives, I am honoring my father, my mother, and also my sister. For many years, I was looking for a way to take what I had learned from my own experiences, both during my father's lifetime and after his death, to help others and carry on his legacy. I was looking for a sign to show me that it was possible to carry on and do good things, the way my father had before me.

I've had a lot of time to sit back and reflect. I've learned a lot about what can make you happy and what can't, chasing some of the things that don't, trying to find happiness in directions that just don't bring it. Having spent a bunch of time alone and then going out and working on the mental health parity bill and getting involved again, I saw that what matters is making a positive difference in life. It's what my father was all about. I've found that compass. It's not about being the best businessperson or having a big house. Some people think they feel empty inside, but if they have a bigger house they might feel better. They don't. Let's put everything into perspective. There is good and bad and suffering all over the world. You're either trying to make a difference or you are part of the problem.

So many people have come up to me over the years and wanted to know, "How did you get through this tragedy?" Mostly, I got through thanks to the love and support of family and friends. One of the things that hit me hard after the crash was the huge importance of connecting with the family I had left, especially my daughter and son, Cari and Keith. But as I've said, Amigo Road and its magic also played a big part in my journey of recovery. Being connected with the earth and the outdoors—those real things that matter—had a tonic effect on me.

This was the start of my own journey of healing, but if I thought that journey had come to an end, then that would not speak too well for me, would it? No, it's an ongoing journey. If anything, I feel that I'm early on that path, that I have much more work to do, much more discovery and learning ahead, but now I've come to the fun part—the part of helping others, giving something back, bringing people along with me to explore how they, too, can find more meaning in their lives.

It was not until I started working on this book that I really started to feel that I had made that transition forward. I'd thought of doing a book for years, of course. People were always telling me I needed to put down some stories about my old man. The time never felt right. But as my kids got older—Cari off at San Francisco State and Keith in his senior year of high school, ready to go off to college—I started to get an itch. I knew I'd need some help telling my story, but had no idea how that would work or who I could ever trust enough to let inside my head that way.

That's when Steve and Sarah came up to see me one afternoon at the Amigo Road house. I was not sure what to expect. Steve, a former reporter for *New York Newsday* and the *San Francisco Chronicle,* has published a lot of books as an author, editor, ghostwriter, and book doctor, including three *New York Times* best-sellers. Sarah, who grew up near Nuremberg, earned her master's degree in international relations and has wide experience working with international nonprofit organizations in Kosovo and elsewhere in the Balkans. Within half an hour of meeting, the three of us were swept up in the energy of the idea that three people from different backgrounds with a common vision and passion could unite toward one goal: turning the Amigo Road house I had worked on for years into a place of healing and sanctuary and founding it as a Wellstone Center in the Redwoods, where we could bring a few people at a time to be energized and renewed through workshops and other programs, from weekend writing workshops to fun-in-the-California-redwoods weekends for couples or for longtime friends looking to renew or regenerate an important friendship. In other words, let the special environment of Amigo

Road open up people's hearts and imaginations and help them move toward making meaningful changes in their own lives— and to better be able to work for social change generally.

Trying to bring those plans to life is a major focus for me now. Good intentions are great—an important first step in getting anywhere—but good intentions alone count for nothing. As my father always emphasized, what matters most is getting down to the hard work of really living your life the way you wish you could live it. There is no tomorrow. There is no "if only." There is only working to live up to your ideals and your dreams. I'd always hoped that the Amigo Road house would become a special place where people could visit for years to come, even if I moved back to Minnesota; a place where people could come to feel a deep sense of calm and perspective and have a chance to walk along private trails through the redwoods or watch the hummingbirds buzz by with the glassy glare of the Pacific Ocean a few miles in the background, sun shining, light breeze smelling of both redwood and salt air. Now we are working to bring those plans to life, including creating residencies where writers of diverse backgrounds can stay at Amigo Road for a week or two or longer and tap the creative energy of the environment to help them make progress on their writing and the social good that writing can accomplish. But most of all, we are working to create a place where the kind of hopeful, healing conversation that flowed so naturally between the three of us, with new ideas popping out every few minutes, could flow between a larger circle of people, and they could be nourished and regenerated through that conversation.

Writing a book, it turns out, is really just having a conversation. That's what we're doing right here, sharing ideas, you and me. Oh, maybe there was a time when books were supposed to be all about wise men talking down to people. Those days are gone. You can and should talk back. Visit the book website at www.becomingwellstone.com or its Facebook page, also called Becoming Wellstone. Have I inspired you at all? Made you laugh once or twice? If so, please tell me about it. People think authors are so busy and don't want to hear from them, but that is so, so wrong. You kidding me? I'm still amazed I've written this book. I'm dying to get started on the part I've been looking forward to all this time, me the guy who can't sit still, and that's getting out and about and talking to people in person about their experience of reading the book and what impact, if any, it might have had.

Let's work together to come up with answers to the problems we all know we face. How do we channel the example of those who have inspired us in a way that moves us forward, against the enemies of apathy and negativity, cynicism and drift, and try to engage ourselves day in and day out in making a difference? I don't claim to have all the answers on that. I'm not sure I have any answers, just a passionate dedication to looking for answers. Help me with that.

My dad always taught me that people working together can make a huge, amazing difference, so help me now to come up with some answers. Help me now to get people excited about the chance to make a difference, whether it's volunteering to work with some disadvantaged kids, giving up bad habits and living a healthier life, or getting involved with the Wellstone Center in the Redwoods.

"There is one lesson that I have learned that I hold above all others from my experience as a father, teacher, community organizer, and U.S. senator: We should never separate the lives we live from the words we speak," my father wrote in *The Conscience of a Liberal.* "To me, the most important goal is to live a life consistent with the values I hold dear and to act on what I believe in."[29]

This book is an account of a journey. I've asked you all along on that journey with me. But the journey is ongoing. I'm just getting going. I want to come to your community—and yours and yours. If you can organize a few people to come on over for some snacks and conversation, and you'd like me to come talk about my book, I'd love to do it. Email us at becomingwellstone@gmail.com and we'd be happy to do our best to organize that. I plan to visit hundreds of living rooms in the months ahead, once this book is published. It's what my old man would have done.

AFTERWORD

by Jim Ramstad

Dave Wellstone has honored his father's legacy with "Wellstone grit" and perseverance in helping secure passage of the landmark Paul Wellstone and Pete Domenici Mental Health Parity and Addiction Equity Act of 2008. Working with Dave Wellstone to pass this legislation was like working with Paul. Like his dad, Dave Wellstone is high energy, hard working, and highly skilled in the ways of Capitol Hill. Also like his dad, Dave has a big heart for people suffering the ravages of mental illness and addiction. Just as I valued Paul Wellstone as a colleague and friend, I also value his son David as a friend and ally in our effort to treat diseases of the brain the same as diseases of the body.

I will always be grateful that I had the opportunity to work with Senator Paul and Sheila Wellstone on the mental illness and addiction parity legislation, as well as the Violence Against Women Act, among other important legislation, and I will forever appreciate their friendship, despite our political differences.

Dave Wellstone embodies the fighting spirit, concern for the less fortunate, and great sense of humor of both his beloved parents. Paul and Sheila would be proud of both their sons, Dave and Mark, who have honored their parents' legacy with courage and determination in the face of great loss. Although it's been ten years since that tragic plane crash claimed the lives of Paul, Sheila, and sister Marcia, among others, I still mourn their loss.

Frequently, when Paul and I would appear together at various meetings and forums, he would exclaim, "Ramstad, I love you like a brother, but how can you be so wrong?!" Then he would laugh uproariously and slap me on the back. That was Paul. He never took himself too seriously, but was very serious in fighting for the causes he championed.

Following the fatal plane crash, David Wellstone picked up the mantra of his father and worked tirelessly and at great personal expense to win support for the mental health and addiction parity legislation. I know it was painful for Dave to leave his new home in California to fly frequently to Washington to lobby Congress and speak at hearings and rallies for the parity bill. But like his dad, Dave always answered the call to duty.

Dave Wellstone was truly instrumental in securing passage of the life-saving treatment parity legislation. Testifying at Congressional hearings with former First Lady Rosalynn Carter or knocking on the doors of Congress, Dave showed the same passion, tenacity, and eloquence that characterized his father's service in the United States Senate.

As chief co-sponsors of the mental health parity bill that ultimately passed Congress and was signed into law by President George W. Bush in October of 2008, Congressman Patrick Kennedy and I will always be grateful for the important role of David Wellstone in winning this twelve-year legislative battle. Congress honored the memory of Senator Paul Wellstone by enacting this landmark mental health law which will always carry Paul's name as the original author.

The Mental Health Parity and Addiction Equity Act of 2008 requires health plans to cover mental illnesses and addiction the same as other health conditions. An estimated 100 million Americans will benefit from equitable coverage under the law. As a grateful recovering alcoholic myself, I am alive and sober today, in large part, because of the access I had to treatment. Unfortunately, millions of Americans suffering from mental disorders and addiction have been denied such access to treatment. It's time to treat diseases of the brain the same as diseases of the body with regard to insurance coverage. It's time to eliminate the discrimination in treatment and the stigma associated with mental illness and addiction. And, it's time to honor the legacy of Senator Paul Wellstone and pay tribute to the good work of his son David in helping to enact the Paul Wellstone and Pete Domenici Mental Health Parity and Addiction Equity Act of 2008.

Jim Ramstad, R-Minn., served in the U.S. House of Representatives from 1991 to 2009.

APPENDIX

PAUL WELLSTONE OBITUARY

from the *New York Times*

A DEATH IN THE SENATE: The Senator Paul Wellstone, 58, Icon of Liberalism in Senate

By David E. Rosenbaum

Published: October 26, 2002

Paul Wellstone often seemed out of step. He called himself a liberal when many used that word as a slur. He voted against the Persian Gulf war in his first year in the Senate, and this month opposed using force against Iraq.

Senator Wellstone, 58, who died in a plane crash today while campaigning for re-election, fought for bills favored by unions and advocates of family farmers and the poor, and against those favored by banks, agribusiness and large corporations.

This year he was the principal opponent of legislation supported by large majorities of Democrats and Republicans that would make it more difficult for people to declare bankruptcy. He argued that the measure would enrich creditors at the expense of people "in brutal economic circumstances." He advocated causes like national health insurance that even many of his fellow liberals abandoned as futile.

Mr. Wellstone was a rumpled, unfailingly modest man who, unlike many of his colleagues, lived on his Senate salary. He was married to the former Sheila Ison for 39 years, having married at 19 when he was in college. His wife and their 33-year-old daughter, Marcia, also died today in the crash.

When Mr. Wellstone arrived in the Senate in 1991, he was a firebrand who thought little of breaking the Senate tradition of comity and personally attacking his colleagues. He told an interviewer soon after he was elected that Senator Jesse Helms, the conservative North Carolina Republican, "represents everything to me that is ugly and wrong and awful about politics."

But as the years passed, Mr. Wellstone moderated his personality if not his politics and became well liked by Republicans as well as Democrats. Bob Dole, the former Senate Republican leader who often tangled with Mr. Wellstone on legislation, choked up today when he told a television interviewer that Mr. Wellstone was "a decent, genuine guy who had a different philosophy from almost everyone else in the Senate."

Mr. Wellstone was also an accomplished campaigner. Though he had never held elected office, he pulled off a major upset in 1990 when, running on a shoestring budget, he defeated the incumbent Republican senator, Rudy Boschwitz. He beat Mr. Boschwitz in a rematch in 1996. This year, he reneged on a promise to limit himself to two terms, ran for re-election and seemed in the most recent public polls to have pulled slightly ahead of his Republican challenger, former Mayor Norm Coleman of St. Paul.

His opponents always portrayed him as a left-wing extremist. Mr. Boschwitz's television commercials in 1996 called Mr. Wellstone "embarrassingly liberal and out of touch." This year, Mr. Coleman said the senator was "so far out of the mainstream, so extreme, that he can't deliver for Minnesotans."

But on the campaign trail, Mr. Wellstone appeared to be so happy, so comfortable, so unthreatening that he was able to ward off the attacks.

For years, he had walked with a pronounced limp that he attributed to an old wrestling injury. In February, he announced at a news conference that he had learned he had multiple sclerosis, but he said the illness would not affect his campaigning or his ability to sit in the Senate. "I have a strong mind—although there are some that might disagree about that—I have a strong body, I have a strong heart, I have a strong soul," he told reporters.

Paul David Wellstone was born in Washington on July 21, 1944, and grew up in Arlington, Va. His father, Leon, left Russia as a child to escape the persecution of Jews, and worked as a writer for the United States Information Agency. His mother, Minnie, the daughter of immigrants from Russia, worked in a junior high school cafeteria.

Growing up, he was more interested in wrestling than politics, and he had some difficulty in school because of what he later found out was a learning disability. He scored lower than 800, out of a total of 1,600, on his College Boards, and this led him as a senator to oppose measures that emphasized standardized test scores. In an interview, he once said that even as an adult he had difficulty interpreting charts and graphs quickly but that he had learned to overcome his disability by studying harder and taking more time to absorb information.

Partly because of his wrestling ability—he was a conference champion at 126 pounds—he was admitted to the University of North Carolina and, galvanized by the civil rights movement, he turned from wrestling to politics. He graduated in 1965 and stayed in Chapel Hill for a doctorate in political science. He wrote his thesis on the roots of black militancy.

Married with children, he once said he did not have time to participate in the student uprisings in the 1960's. He is survived by two grown sons, David and Mark, of St. Paul, and six grandchildren.

But while he was not a student rebel, Mr. Wellstone did not fit in from the day in 1969 when he began teaching political science at Carleton College, a small liberal arts campus in rural Northfield, Minn.

He was more interested in leading his students in protests than he was in publishing in academic journals, and he was often at odds with his colleagues and Carleton administrators. He fought the college's investments in companies doing business in South Africa, battled local banks that foreclosed on farms, picketed with strikers at a meat-packing plant and taught classes off campus rather than cross a picket line when Carleton's custodians were on strike.

In 1974, the college told him his contract would not be renewed. But with strong support from students, the student newspaper and local activists, he appealed the dismissal, and it was reversed.

In 1982, Mr. Wellstone dipped his toe into the political waters for the first time and ran for state auditor. He lost. But he had made contacts in the Minnesota Democratic-Farmer-Labor Party, and he stayed active in politics. In 1988, he was the state co-chairman of the Rev. Jesse Jackson's campaign in the presidential primary, and in the general election, he was co-chairman of the campaign of Michael S. Dukakis, the Democratic presidential nominee.

Few thought he had a chance when he announced that he would run for the Senate against Mr. Boschwitz. Russell D. Feingold, now a like-minded liberal Democratic senator from Wisconsin, today had this recollection of dropping by to meet Mr. Wellstone in 1989:

"He opened the door, and there he was with his socks off, 15 books open that he was reading, and he was on the phone arguing with somebody about Cuba. He gave me coffee, and we laughed uproariously at the idea that either of us would ever be elected. But he pulled it off in 1990 and gave me the heart to do it in Wisconsin."

Mr. Feingold was elected in 1992, also with a tiny treasury.

Mr. Boschwitz spent $7 million on his campaign, seven times Mr. Wellstone's budget. To counteract the Boschwitz attacks, Mr. Wellstone ran witty, even endearing television commercials produced without charge by a group led by a former student. In one ad, the video and audio were speeded up, and Mr. Wellstone said he had to talk fast because "I don't have $6 million to spend."

Mr. Wellstone toured the state in a battered green school bus, and in the end, he won 50.4 percent of the vote and was the only challenger in 1990 to defeat an incumbent senator.

He arrived in Washington as something of a rube. On one of his first days in town before he was sworn in, he called a reporter for the name of a restaurant where he could get a cheap dinner. When the reporter replied that he knew a place where a good meal was only $15, Mr. Wellstone said $15 was many times what he was prepared to spend.

He also made what he later conceded were "rookie mistakes." At one point, for instance, he used the Vietnam Veterans Memorial as a backdrop for a news conference to oppose the war against Iraq. Veterans' groups denounced him, and he later apologized.

But he soon warmed to the ways of the Senate and became especially adept at the unusual custom of giving long speeches to an empty chamber. Probably no one in the Senate over the last dozen years gave more speeches at night after nearly all the other senators had gone home.

His strength was not in getting legislation enacted. One successful measure he sponsored in 1996 with Senator Pete V. Domenici, Republican of New Mexico, requires insurance companies in some circumstances to give coverage to people with mental illness, but he failed this year in an effort to strengthen the law.

In a book he published last year, "The Conscience of a Liberal" (Random House), Mr. Wellstone wrote, "I feel as if 80 percent of my work as a senator has been playing defense, cutting the extremist enthusiasms of the conservative agenda (much of which originates in the House) rather than moving forward on a progressive agenda."

In a speech in the Senate this month explaining his opposition to the resolution authorizing the use of force in Iraq, Mr. Wellstone stressed that Saddam Hussein was "a brutal, ruthless dictator who has repressed his own people."

But Mr. Wellstone went on to say: "Despite a desire to support our president, I believe many Americans still have profound questions about the wisdom of relying too heavily on a pre-emptive go-it-alone military approach. Acting now on our own might be a sign of our power. Acting sensibly and in a measured way, in concert with our allies, with bipartisan Congressional support, would be a sign of our strength."

Later, Mr. Wellstone told a reporter that he did not believe his stance would hurt him politically. "What would really hurt," he said, "is if I was giving speeches and I didn't even believe what I was saying. Probably what would hurt is if people thought I was doing something just for political reasons."

Mr. Wellstone briefly considered running for president in 2000, but he called off the campaign because, he said, the doctors who had been treating him for a ruptured disk told him that his back could not stand the travel that would be required.

Often, Mr. Wellstone was the only senator voting against a measure, or one of only a few. He was, for instance, one of three senators in 1999 to support compromise missile defense legislation. He was the only one that year to vote against an education bill involving standardized tests, and the only Democrat who opposed his party's version of lowering the estate tax.

Mr. Wellstone was one of the few senators who made the effort to meet and remember the names of elevator operators, waiters, police officers and other workers in the Capitol.

James W. Ziglar, a Republican who was sergeant at arms of the Senate from 1998 to 2001 and who is now commissioner of the Immigration and Naturalization Service, remembered today "the evening when he came back to the Capitol well past midnight to visit with the cleaning staff and tell them how much he appreciated their efforts."

"Most of the staff had never seen a senator and certainly had never had one make such a meaningful effort to express his or her appreciation," Mr. Ziglar said. "That was the measure of the man."

TRANSCRIPT OF
DAVE WELLSTONE'S EULOGY

Given at the Memorial Service
for Paul Wellstone

University of Minnesota
October 29, 2002

What I decided to do was I wanted to just pick a few words that came to my mind as it related to my sister, my father, and my mother, tell a few things about them that really . . . [I] could go on forever. I could sit up here all night . . . I've got a little bit of my dad in me in that respect. But I'm going to try and keep it short.

I'm going to start with my sister, Marcia, who I love dearly. "Loving," "energetic," and "beautiful" were three words that came to my mind. Marcia became a very good friend to me. We had four years' difference [in age], but in recent years we'd gone through some similar events. I found her to be one of my closest confidants and somebody I could go to, and I really miss that about her already. Her infectious smile— that most of you who had seen her know—lit the faces of others. And that's going to be missed. The machine-gun laugh that some of you may know about . . . I wish I could imitate it, but I can't . . . that laugh made me smile. Her ability to connect with others, which was mentioned earlier . . . it's amazing. And it's been indicated by all the close friends she has, everywhere she's gone she's made friends that are close, just like her friends out here. Her love and devotion to her son, Josh, was unparalleled. Her love and devotion to her husband, Todd, was unparalleled. When I looked at the two of them together, I thought, *Wow. It can't get much better than that.*

When I was in the first grade, I was short, even though I am the tallest in the family by a couple of inches. And being small, I was bullied. And I'll never forget, I used to come home from school crying, and finally my dad happened to get home from class—he was teaching at Carleton at the time—and he said, "What's wrong?" And I said, "I've got these bullies." And he said, "We'll take care of that." The next day, he waited outside the school behind a tree, and he watched what went on. He came over and—let me just put it this way—he took care of it. Never again would I have to worry about that stuff.

Things that some of you may not know, that I can remember, our OBRC, Organization for a Better Rice County, when he was a college teacher . . . organizing, organizing, always organizing. He always had social justice in his bones. The powerline struggle in west central Minnesota . . . I remember going out with him while those farmers were fighting that line that came across. Baseball at the old Met . . . one of my fondest memories with my dad. In more recent years, I enjoyed the political strategy discussions we had, and I enjoyed working with him in 1990 and 1996. I was looking forward to these last weeks. And I'm still looking forward to digging in in his name.

One of the things that stands out the most about my dad is that it did not matter what was going on [with himself] . . . he was concerned about others. The MS, neck surgery, all the other things, he was not concerned about himself. He was concerned about his family and how they would react. And I think that's a very special quality. The values he instilled in us as kids growing up, I would say, were rooted more in social justice and doing the right thing than anything else. And, certain words in our house—you know, swear words and curse words—I'll tell you the kind of words you never uttered in our house, and those would be disparaging words about somebody of a different ethnic group, of a different color, of a different sex, or of a different orientation. And you know how it is, kids do what you do, not what you say, and he led by example. And I appreciate that.

He was a wonderful father and a wonderful grandfather. He was always there when you needed him. One thing about my dad [was] when the going got rough, when you really, really needed him, there's no one else you wanted in your corner. That's for us personally, and for everybody in this state.

The synergy my dad had with my mom was unbelievable, and that's how I want to leave my words about my dad is that my parents were inseparable. My father loved my mother more than anything, and my mother loved my father more than anything. And if there's any solace to be taken, [it is] that they passed away together along with my sister—they're together. And that's the way it should've been.

I need to talk about my mom last, because my mom held everything together. My mom was everything to us. My dad wasn't who he was without my mom. The words that came to my mind when I thought about my mother were "selfless," "loving," "caring," "tenacious," "proud," "beautiful," and here on my little chicken-scrabble sheet I underlined "strong," because that's what she was.

My mom and I were very close. These are the things I remember most about her: coffee together, lunch together, my deepest fears, concerns, joys, asking for advice. My mom was always there with the best. Buddy Holly . . . she loved Buddy Holly. She gave of herself like you wouldn't believe. She was selfless. I remember my mom taking care of me when I was sick . . . the wet washcloth on the forehead, all those nurturing things. It's just too hard to talk about them all.

I watched my mom go from being an assistant librarian and raising us. She did everything. She cooked meals, she got us to school, she went to work, she came home, she went to sporting events, she cooked dinner. Oh, and by the way, we didn't all like the same food, so she cooked a little of this, a little of that, and [she would] say, "Oh, honey, sorry, I'll make you a hamburger." That's the kind of mother she was. I watched her go from raising us to becoming a powerhouse in her own right, equal to my father. Whether it was domestic abuse or all the other issues my father championed, she was there with him.

Those who know my mom and my dad know that they got things done. I've heard others say they didn't get anything done, and I say, "Ignorance is bliss." They got things done, and they changed untold lives forever. And I know that, and I know you know that, and I know their colleagues know that. The legacy and the beliefs and the vision of my dad we all know, whether you agree with him or not. And I believe, with all my heart, that that legacy will carry on in Minnesota, it will carry on in this country, and it will carry on throughout the world. And we know what we need to do to make that happen.

I want to end my remarks with just a quick story. I don't know how long ago it was, my dad had come home from the Red Lake Indian Reservation and he said, "I was getting ready to speak. And just as I got up there, the spiritual leader came up to me and said 'The eagle passed by as you were up there. That's a very good sign.'"

And then, we went to the crash site the other day. And as we were leaving that site, I saw this huge, white ball on the road, and then it flew up into the tree and sat there, and as we went by we looked, and it was a huge bald eagle perched there looking out over us.

Make of it what you want, but I'll tell you what I think. I think that my father, my mother, my sister, and all the others are there looking over us. Thank you for coming. Thank you for loving my father.

The Paul Wellstone
and Pete Domenici Mental Health Parity
and Addiction Equity Act of 2008

The Paul Wellstone and Pete Domenici Mental Health Parity and Addiction Equity Act (MHPAEA) was passed into law in 2008 to correct discriminatory health care practices against those with a mental illness and/or addiction. This groundbreaking, bipartisan law expands access to treatment by prohibiting most insurance plans from restricting coverage or imposing unequal limitations on treatment options if they provide mental health or addiction coverage. In other words, if they offer mental health and addiction benefits, they must be provided "on par" with medical benefits covered under the plan. Significantly, the law aims to curb both the financial and nonfinancial or "nonquantitative" ways that plans limit access to addiction and mental health care. The law applies to self-insured and large employer group plans, but not to individual or small group plans. Leaders like Senator Wellstone worked together with individuals with mental illness and/or addiction, their families, professionals in the field, and employers to pass this important law. The following is an excerpt:

In the case of a group health plan (or health insurance coverage offered in connection with such a plan) that provides both medical and surgical benefits and mental health or substance use disorder benefits, such plan or coverage shall ensure that—

(i) the financial requirements applicable to such mental health or substance use disorder benefits are no more restrictive than the predominant financial requirements applied to substantially all medical and surgical benefits covered by the plan (or coverage), and there are no separate cost sharing requirements that are applicable only with respect to mental health or substance use disorder benefits; and

(ii) the treatment limitations applicable to such mental health or substance use disorder benefits are no more restrictive than the predominant treatment limitations applied to substantially all medical and surgical benefits covered by the plan (or coverage) and there are no separate treatment limitations that are applicable only with respect to mental health or substance use disorder benefits.

Pub. L. No. 110-343, 122 Stat. 3881 (2008)

NOTES

1. Ronald Smothers, "Welfare Activist Plans New Group; Will Leave Rights Post for Economic Justice Drive," *New York Times,* December 17, 1972.

2. Paul Wellstone, *The Conscience of a Liberal: Reclaiming the Compassionate Agenda* (New York: Random House, 2001), 6.

3. Dennis J. McGrath and Dane Smith, *Professor Wellstone Goes to Washington* (Minneapolis: University of Minnesota Press, 1995), 3.

4. Doris Grumbach, *New York Times Book Review,* June 11, 1978.

5. Ibid.

6. "The 1990 Elections; Primary Results: Setting the Stage for November," *New York Times,* September 13, 1990; www.nytimes.com/1990/09/13/us/the-1990-elections-primary -results-setting-the-stage-for-november.html?pagewanted =all&src=pm.

7. Eric Black, "Mondale Close to Yes," *Minneapolis Star Tribune,* October 27, 2002; www.startribune.com/politics /11763066.html?page=all&prepage=4&c=y.

8. Walter Mondale with David Hage, *The Good Fight: A Life in Liberal Politics* (New York: Scribner, 2010), 333.

9. Harriet Barovick, "Washington's Latter Day Mr. Smith," *Time,* December 22, 2002.

10. www.now.org/history/wellstone-tributes.html.

11. Tom Daschle, *Like No Other Time: The 107th Congress and the Two Years That Changed America* (New York: Crown Publishers, Inc., 2003), 253–4.

12. "Birds of a Feather," *Northern Exposure,* CBS, 11/1/93.

13. Deborah Sontag, "When Politics Is Personal," *New York Times,* September 15, 2002.

14. Ibid.

15. Paul Kane, "Carrying On His Father's Fight," *Roll Call* November 6, 2003.

16. Carol McDaid, personal interview, April 2012.

17. Ibid.

18. www.cartercenter.org/news/editorials_speeches/rosalynn _mhtestimony.html

19. Ibid.

20. From the Hearing before the Subcommittee on Health, Employment, Labor and Pensions, Committee on Education and Labor, July 10, 2007; www.gpo.gov/fdsys /pkg/CHRG-110hhrg36468/pdf/CHRG -110hhrg36468.pdf.

21. Michael Duffy, "After the Financial Crisis a Cleanup That Changes Everything," *Time,* September 22, 2008.

22. Jackie Calmes, "In Bailout Vote, a Leadership Breakdown," *New York Times,* September 29, 2008.

23. "Oh So Close to Mental Health Parity," *New York Times* editorial, October 1, 2008.

24. Tony Fratto, Press Briefing, Office of the Press Secretary, September 29, 2008; http://georgewbush-whitehouse .archives.gov/news/releases/2008/09/20080929-7.html.

25. Edmund L. Andrews and Mark Landler, "Treasury and Fed Looking at Options," *New York Times,* September 29, 2008; www.nytimes.com/2008/09/30/business/30plan.html?_r=1.

26. Robert Pear, "Bailout Provides More Mental Health Coverage," *New York Times,* October 5, 2008.

27. Carol McDaid, personal interview, April 2012.

28. Fred Frommer, "After 12 Years, Mental Health Parity Act Is Law," Associated Press, October 3, 2008.

29. Wellstone, *Conscience of a Liberal,* ix.

ABOUT THE AUTHOR

Paul David Wellstone Jr., son of Senator Paul Wellstone, is the founding partner of Family Place Home Builders, a business dedicated to building affordable housing. He resides in St. Paul, Minnesota, with his wife Leah. A graduate of Hamline University, Dave is a founder, with his brother Mark, of Wellstone Action, and founder of a new nonprofit devoted to mental-health parity issues. He is a cofounder of the Wellstone Center in the Redwoods, www.wellstone redwoods.org, located amid the spectacular beauty of the Santa Cruz Mountains in California, which seeks to promote an atmosphere of tranquility and calm and to bolster the talents and capabilities of people through workshops, seminars, and residencies. Dave will be leading workshops on this book at the Center.

PHOTO CREDITS

The photos on the chapter openers are credited to the following:

Prologue: *AP Photo/M. Spencer Green*

Chapter 1: *Author photo*

Chapter 2: *Author photo*

Chapter 3: *Author photo*

Chapter 4: *Tom Sweeney/Star Tribune*

Chapter 5: *Author photo*

Chapter 6: *AP Photo/Dennis Cook*

Chapter 7: *AP Photo/Manuel Balce Cenata*

Chapter 8: *AP Photo/Mesabi Daily News, Mark Sauer*

Conclusion: *Author photo*